F   *Society*

"What you hold in your hands is a unique book. I honestly know of none quite like it. But its uniqueness should not be interpreted as novel or niche; this book is of the utmost importance. Faith and pluralism have become (at times tensely) linked in late modernity. It is nearly impossible—at least in the Western world—to imagine one without the other. Our young people, perhaps even more than adults, feel both the possibilities and problems with this linking. It then is a great gift to have before us *Youth Ministry in a Multifaith Society*. It promises to deepen your perspective and practice of youth ministry, and challenge you at every turn. Embrace it as the gift it is."

Andrew Root, author of *Revisiting Relational Youth Ministry*

"A timely, much-needed perspective on the challenges of ministry in multifaith societies. The text is content-rich and globally aware, pulling together many threads of research into one seamless must-read book for thinking youth workers."

Andy du Feu, director of youth and community work, Moorlands College, Christchurch, UK

"Len Kageler's new book vacuumed me in—and I carefully read every line. I will continue to grieve over the growing percentage of people who don't know Jesus, but Len opened my eyes to opportunities in this environment. What a wonderful time to show teenagers how to love without conditions, to understand how the truth claims of the Christian faith are distinct from other systems and to grasp much more of the entirely unique Son of God so their hearts will intertwine with his forever."

Richard Ross, professor of student ministry, Southwestern Seminary

"For the first time, this book shows youth workers how to ground their young people in their faith while encouraging their relationships with friends of other faiths. Anyone involved in youth ministry will treasure this book because it provides another avenue to help youth workers become reflective, observant and engaged in doing youth ministry in a multifaith society."

Rev. Nathan H. Chiroma, lecturer in youth ministry and Christian education, ECWA Theological Seminary, Jos, Nigeria

"After reading this book, one will consider one's own views on pluralism and approaches in youth ministry from a christological point of view. This is an informative and relevant book for the contexts of Europe and the United States. I highly recommend it."

Rev. Ronelle Sonnenberg, Protestant Church in the Netherlands, coordinator of the Research Centre for Youth, Church, and Culture

"With a contagious passion for both quantitative research and Christology, and particularly the challenging interrelationship between the two, Len Kageler invites Christian youth ministers around the globe to rethink youth ministry in a multifaith society. Although writing out of a North American context, Kageler offers thoughtful reflections, insights and ideas that may prove helpful for youth ministers in other parts of the world who are faithfully seeking to develop a pastoral theology for youth ministry in an emerging multifaith society."

Bård Eirik Hallesby Norheim, associate professor of practical theology, NLA University College, Bergen, Norway

"A timely and relevant resource. . . . This book would greatly aid youth ministers, professors and Christian educators in establishing our students in the faith, while ministering to those whose faiths are different or nonexistent."

Anne De Jesus-Ardina, faculty/director for youth studies and Christian education, Alliance Graduate School, Metro Manila, Philippines

"We all need this book written by an active youth minister and vigilant scholar. Its topic has been largely ignored; its research and theology are compelling. Kageler's data on Muslim youth ministry alone makes looking into this work worthwhile, but there's more. Who's gaining and who's losing across the religious field? How does Christ win in multifaith contexts? How does all this work out in practical youth ministry? The book's answers make this a must for youth pastors' libraries."

Dean Borgman, director, Center for Youth Studies, Gordon-Conwell Theological Seminary

Youth Ministry

in a Multifaith

Society

**FORMING CHRISTIAN IDENTITY AMONG
SKEPTICS, SYNCRETISTS AND SINCERE
BELIEVERS OF OTHER FAITHS**

LEN KAGELER
FOREWORD BY CHAP CLARK

IVP Books

An imprint of InterVarsity Press
Downers Grove, Illinois

InterVarsity Press
P.O. Box 1400, Downers Grove, IL 60515-1426
World Wide Web: www.ivpress.com
Email: email@ivpress.com

InterVarsity Press® is the book-publishing division of InterVarsity Christian Fellowship/USA®, a movement of students and faculty active on campus at hundreds of universities, colleges and schools of nursing in the United States of America, and a member movement of the International Fellowship of Evangelical Students. For information about local and regional activities, write Public Relations Dept., InterVarsity Christian Fellowship/USA, 6400 Schroeder Rd., P.O. Box 7895, Madison, WI 53707-7895, or visit the IVCF website at www.intervarsity.org.

All Scripture quotations, unless otherwise indicated, are taken from THE HOLY BIBLE, NEW INTERNATIONAL VERSION®, NIV® Copyright © 1973, 1978, 1984, 2011 by Biblica, Inc.™ Used by permission. All rights reserved worldwide.

While all stories in this book are true, some names and identifying information in this book have been changed to protect the privacy of the individuals involved.

Cover design: David Fassett
Interior design: Beth Hagenberg
Images: wrist bracelet: Medioimages/Photodisc/Getty Images
    Darwin and Christian fish symbol: © quisp65/iStockphoto
    religious symbols: © pop_jop/iStockphoto
    WWJD bracelet: © hannahgleg/iStockphoto

ISBN 978-0-8308-4112-7 (print)
ISBN 978-0-8308-8407-0 (digital)

Printed in the United States of America ∞

Library of Congress Cataloging-in-Publication Data
A catalog record for this book is available from the Library of Congress.

P   21   20   19   18   17   16   15   14   13   12   11   10   9   8   7   6   5   4   3   2   1

Y   32   31   30   29   28   27   26   25   24   23   22   21   20   19   18   17   16   15   14

To four colleagues who each, in their own way,
have blessed me, stretched me and inspired me:

Colin Bennett, Moorlands College, UK
Kenda Creasy Dean, Princeton Seminary, US
Andrew Root, Luther Seminary, US
Pete Ward, Kings College, UK

CONTENTS

FOREWORD

During my early years of teaching—at Denver Seminary, one of the first standalone youth ministry masters programs in the United States—I got a phone call from a representative of a nonevangelical (most Protestants would say "non-Christian") youth ministry organization. They wanted me to come and speak at their annual convention. Mike Yaconelli, the cofounder of Youth Specialties, had spoken the previous year. "He was great. He said you would be exactly what we need to help us think through what it means to do what you evangelicals have been doing for years."

It was a really, really tough dilemma for me. On the one hand, I believed that the gospel proclaimed would shine when lined up alongside what I considered to be extrabiblical doctrine. If I preached Jesus Christ, and him crucified, then what was the harm?

On the other hand, from a practical and purely pragmatic perspective, I was worried about making this group "better" at doing youth ministry. If I were to train them as I would any denomination— if I helped them to see the power of authentic, incarnational relationships, leadership development, speaking to kids and so on—was I helping them to perpetuate what I believed was, in the final analysis, destructive to kids' understanding of historical faith?

At the time, I declined. And now, twenty-plus years later, I regret that decision.

I grew up in youth ministry. I was a product of a parachurch program at my school (Young Life); my leaders there convinced me that to sustain my new faith I needed to get involved in a church. "Youth groups" were the rage at the time—a concerted effort to reintroduce young people to the church. Youth pastors who could play guitar, hold a crowd with humor and passion, and run a good camp or choir were the order of the day.

Central to the thinking then was a conviction that teenagers needed a place where they could be themselves. Throughout the 1970s and into the mid-1980s, youth ministry (usually centered around the youth group) offered a "safe place" for kids to explore their faith, their friendships and the day-to-day experiences that were now part of growing up in a more intense, sexual and "wild living" culture.

Much has been written and debated over how the Christian, primarily Protestant, way of leading and loving kids evolved from there. Certainly there have been spin-offs of perspective, from the strong emphasis on programming during the 1980s (and ever since), to the youth and family ministry movement of the 1990s and the spirituality push of the new millennium. Through it all the "big dog" of youth ministry was what could be broadly described as the evangelical church. Youth Specialties and Group, magazines, books, conventions, seminars and even a movement toward academic degrees helped define and shape a youth ministry movement that belonged solely to "us."

I remember the first time Len Kageler talked to me about this book, or at least the seeds of it. He had stumbled onto something way, way beyond what I did during that phone call: faithful Muslims who, without the training or prompting or even exposure to "our" professional youth ministry community, were doing a great job loving their kids in the name of the God they served. Len had been deeply struck by the integrity and commitment of those who were not supposed to "get it."

After all, "we" had *invented* youth ministry. We were the trainers. We had the history, the writers, the speakers, even the academics.

What could *they* teach *us*? And, more to the point, why should we give them their due?

Len's original vision was to help Christians to realize what was happening in the Muslim world of youth ministry. His motive was to see how we could teach and lead our kids and churches into being global Christians in a pluralistic world without losing our conviction for the gospel of Jesus Christ. A tall order. Marketable? I told Len I loved the idea, and that perhaps the time *had* come when we should realize that lots of people love kids, and love them well—even, in many cases, more deeply than we do. And even more, perhaps the gospel could be better served by being in relationship with those God loves than by being protectionist, defensive or paternalistic.

I have known Len Kageler for years. I know him as a deep thinker, as a sincere and committed trainer of not only youth ministry but Christian leadership, and as a friend who is not afraid to ask any question, so long as it serves the interests and values of God's kingdom. This book is, I believe, better than Len's initial idea, for he goes beyond what Muslims are doing and gets us into what so many others who do not share our theological convictions are discovering and practicing so we can engage our neighbors with grace, tenderness and compassion.

I love this book. I am so grateful for Len and his dogged commitment to moving youth ministry beyond our culture and prototypes to seeking what God is up to in an increasingly smaller world. I am especially thankful that, because of Len and this book, youth ministry leaders and practitioners will be far more inclined to build bridges instead of walls, and even speak to and with those who are outside our sphere and our boxes. I only wish I had had this perspective so many years ago.

Chap Clark
Professor of Youth, Family and Culture
Fuller Theological Seminary

INTRODUCTION

How would you have understood this news item?

University of Chester Announces Their New Muslim Youthwork
Degree Program

I thought to myself, *Oh, that is so interesting! There must be so many
Muslims around Chester, United Kingdom, that Christians are getting
special training on how to reach out to them.*

I was wrong.

My office desk was a mess, and there was not nearly enough time
before my Introduction to Youth Ministry class began to even make
a dent in the pile. So, instead I pulled *Youthwork* off my shelf.
Youthwork is out of the United Kingdom, and I enjoy seeing ministries and resources that represent a non–United States perspective. I
always flip to the news section first.

And there it was, the announcement about a Muslim youth work
degree.

I kept reading and realized my first impression was totally wrong.
This was not a degree program for Christians who wanted to do
youth ministry reaching out to Muslim-background youth, it was a
degree program for Muslims who wanted to do youth work *as
Muslims, for Muslims.*

Now *that* was something I had never thought about before.

This book is about Christian youth ministry done in settings where the religious marketplace is festooned with religious choices other than Christianity. It is also about Christian youth ministry in settings where many choose to have no religious faith of any sort, or if they do, they reduce that faith to the trivial. This book is also about Christian youth ministry in settings where many choose to embrace a religion other than Christianity and are quite happy with their choice, thank you very much.

In addition to being a professor teaching youth ministry, I am also a youth ministry volunteer in a local church, working with young teens. And yes, I'm as old as their grandparents, but they do know I'm in good shape (being a long-distance runner) and can thus pretty much catch up with any of them in any games that involve chasing. And they respect that I have pretty good skills in a couple of video games (at this writing, the *Halo* and the *Call of Duty* series).[1] Our meetings are fairly typical as far as youth group meetings go: some hangout time, some food, some fun, some together time for spiritual teaching, followed by more hangout time.

About once a month I'm the one who leads the teaching time, and I often have the youth write some kind of response or prayer request on a 3 x 5 card, putting their name on that card, and turning in to me at the end. I pray through the cards during the week and follow up as needed. One of those nights we had an especially good attendance (for us) of about thirty kids, many of whom were guests. Two response cards were particularly striking that night. One girl said, "Please pray for my mother, she is the US Ambassador to Pakistan." (I checked later and found it was true, and this "working mom" commuted between New York and Islamabad). While that card and prayer request were striking, not to mention surprising, it was a different response card that riveted me. Jenny's card was striking as well, but not surprising.

"Please pray for my mother, she's a witch."

I knew Jenny and her context well enough to know she was not speaking of her mom being a witch in the sense that her mother was mean-spirited and bossy. Her mother was a witch as in *a practicing witch, part of a local coven of witches in our community.*

Now, throughout my youth ministry years I've known and experienced youth and families who were not Christians. It is just that in this community, the reality of viable alternatives to the Christian faith is more visible. On my way to youth group I pass one mosque, two synagogues, two closed churches and one new age bookstore.

Needless to say this has triggered a lot of reflection in my own heart, thinking about pluralism, functioning in a multifaith society and critiquing my own Christology. I also ask myself if my youth ministry (or anyone's youth ministry, for that matter) really helps young people and their parents have a viable and credible faith in a culture that tends to categorize the importance of religious choices with the same gravitas as choices about shampoo.

In this book we will first seek to unpack what is happening when it comes to other religions and youth ministry. We'll look also at the rise of religious nones and youth who have a pick-and-choose attitude about aspects of faith. The church, and the Abrahamic faith before it, actually has a great deal to contribute to this conversation today when it comes to being people of faith in a multifaith society. We will look at the traditional, modern and postmodern views when it comes to pluralism, and that a person's theology actually matters when it comes to youth ministry praxis and youth ministry outcomes. This is a book of help and hope: help in understanding what is going on, and hope that ministry among nones, syncretists, and students of other faiths is indeed mission possible.

My heart concern, central to the issue of our functioning in ministry within the cultural milieu of this day and for the foreseeable future, is that our Christology is getting fuzzy. This was not very important to me early in my ministry. Now I see it as central to our own thriving in student ministry and seeing students thrive as well. I want the arc of my life's narrative to be one in which I sense God's presence. I also want my life to be one that is often punctuated by God showing up in unmistakable ways. Simply put, when we get our Christology right, both presence and power are the natural outcomes. For me. For my students.

1

THE RISE OF YOUTH MINISTRY IN OTHER RELIGIONS

A Good Thing for
Christian Youth Work?

For better or worse, I receive a lot of opportunities to speak and teach about all kinds of things related to youth and youth ministry. Recently, I led a seminar with the title "Muslim Youth Ministry . . . Coming Your Direction." There were probably seventy-five persons present, two of whom left in a huff after five minutes when they realized I was not "Muslim bashing." About an hour into the presentation I was making the point that in the United Kingdom many youth pastors actually look for opportunities to get Christian and Muslim youth groups together for joint projects (e.g., to raise money for disaster relief). They do this thinking that Christianity "wins" when placed side by side with Islam, and that both Christian and Muslim young people will see this as they become acquainted with one another. (We'll talk a lot more about that notion in chapter two.)

A youth pastor from Michigan raised his hand and said, "Yes, he's right! We have Muslim students showing up in our youth group meetings all the time. After a while many of these Muslim young people will say something like 'Wow, I had no idea Christianity was this good.'" He went on to say, "We didn't understand at first, but we (both adult volunteers and kids in our group) now 'get it' bigtime that there is no concept of grace in Islam, and that it is all a matter of self-effort. We find that over time Muslims in our youth group connect the dots and they're, well, they're astonished really." There were a half dozen other Michigan youth pastors sitting with him and several of them affirmed, "That's what happened in our youth group too. And it has really helped *our* students know and appreciate their faith."

At first hearing, the idea can be a real shocker. I have come to believe the presence of youth and youth ministries from other religions just may well be a *very* good thing for the Christian church, the Christian family and the Christian youth group.

We will first take a look at non-Christian religious youth ministry in the United States and beyond. Many of these same developments are occurring in other Western countries as well. We will also consider the social science research that reveals a tested or challenged faith is better.

OTHER RELIGIONS IN THE UNITED STATES

Demographers, sociologists and cultural anthropologists are fascinated by the mixing of the world's peoples through migration and the global culture spawned by technology. The rise of other religions in the United States is certainly not as huge as in some other countries. For example, in Australia there are now more Buddhists than Baptists, more Muslims than Lutherans, more Hindus than Jews, and four times as many witches than Quakers.[1] In the United States 60 percent of the population will affirm that religion plays an important part of their lives. In France that number is 11 percent.[2] Tracking religious affiliation in the United States is not as straightforward as in many other countries because the US Census does not include any questions about religion. The United Kingdom, for example, routinely includes a religious affiliation question as part of the decinal census.[3] In the United States researchers glean the information not from the census but from General Social Survey (GSS) conducted by the National Opinion Research Center (NORC) of the University of Chicago. NORC uses statistical sampling techniques to arrive at numbers that represent what can be understood as true for the whole country. Many researchers use additional surveys such as the Religious Identification Survey to corroborate or expand the General Social Survey results.[4] See table 1.1 for the most recent GSS based numbers available on US religious affiliation.

So we see there are other religions in America, but do their adherents have any notion or cultural vocabulary parallel or equivalent to the concept of adolescence as we understand it?

Table 1.1. Religious Affiliation of US Population

Christian	78%
none	16.4%
Jewish	1.8%
Buddhist	1.2%
Muslim	0.9%
Hindu	0.6%
other	0.6%
folk religion	0.2%

Source: "Religious Composition by Country," Pew Research Religion & Public Life Project, accessed March 21, 2013, www.pewforum.org /uploadedFiles/Topics/Religious_Affiliation /globalReligion-tables.pdf.

RELIGIONS AND "YOUTH" AS A CULTURAL CONCEPT

French sociologist Michael Mitterauer is most certainly correct in his observation that in all cultures and in all epochs of human existence a span of time known as "youth" has existed.[5] Its beginning and ending markers have varied among cultures, but every culture and every religion has recognized those who are clearly not children but also clearly not adults.

The Bible. A good example of this cultural understanding of "youth" in an ancient context is our own Old and New Testaments. The word *na'ar* is used forty-five times in the Old Testament and is translated as "youth" in our English Bibles. Remarkably, there are twin positions on youth in the Old Testament Scriptures. On the one hand *na ʿar* is a time that people do things they regret later in life. On the other, it is a time to set a positive pattern for life. For example, David implores the Lord, "Do not remember the sins of my youth" (Ps 25:7). Another time the psalmist affirms "Since my youth, God, you have taught me, and to this day I declare your marvelous deeds" (Ps 71:17). Job, whose very bad day turned into a very bad year, speculates about the reason for his sudden misfortune. Looking heavenward with a sigh, he says, "You write down bitter things against me and make me reap the sins of my youth" (Job 13:26). And pity those poor male *na ʿarim*, forty-two of them to be exact, who make the terrible mistake of commenting on the prophet Elisha's lack of hair. Elisha curses those boys in the name of the Lord, whereupon two bears appear and certainly ruin their day (2 Kings 2:23-25).[6]

The twin stance on "youth" carries forward into the New Testament, where the word *neotēs* is used five times and the related words *neōterikos* and *neanias* are used once each. Paul urges Timothy to "flee the evil desires of youth" (2 Tim 2:22) but at the same time encourages him with the words "Don't let anyone look down upon you because you are young, but be an example for the believers" (1 Tim 4:12).[7]

So Christians have a heritage of viewing youth as a specially demarcated time in a person's life. But what about other religions in America? Do they have a term equivalent to the English *youth*? How do these religions conceptualize adolescence and how to they promote and protect the faith of their own sons and daughters? In other words, how do they do youth ministry?

Islam's understanding of childhood and adolescence. In the sacred text of Islam, the Qur'an, two important milestones of maturity are recognized. The term *b'lum* captures the concept of psychological maturity, and *a'sudd*, which is closely associated with it, carries with it the right to conduct business and the duty to fulfill religious obligations,[8] which are (1) the declaration of faith, "There is no God but God and Mohammed is His Prophet," (2) praying five designated times a day, (3) giving alms to the poor, (4) fasting from before sunrise until sunset during the month of Ramadan, and (5) making the pilgrimage to Mecca, if one can afford it.[9] Those who have achieved *b'lum* and *a'sudd* are expected to engage in these five obligations side by side with other adults in the community.

The Arabic language contains four additional words, not found in the Qur'an, that cumulatively define "youth" or adolescence. *Bulugh* is the Arabic equivalent to the English concept of puberty. It refers also to the growth of pubic hair and the distinctive smell of the armpit of both sexes. Once a young person begins to evidence reflective reason and discernment, he or she is gaining *'aql*.[10] The person who is acquiring *'aql* can see his or her self acting in relation to others. However, this rise of social self-awareness, which is so prominent in Western theories of adolescence, is of only minor importance in Arab cultures, where the primary focus is family, kin and one's place in this constellation of primary relationships.[11] A further term in the Arabic language, *rush'd*, captures the attainment of "reason guided maturity of thought and action, particularly in religious and moral matters."[12] One who is growing in the attainment of *rush'd* is seen more as an adult than as (the fourth Arabic term) *shabb* (youth).[13] The conceptual framework for understanding and describing youth exists, then, in the Arabic language and in Islam. Yetkin Yildirim summarizes Islamic theology:

> Islam teaches that every child is born sinless and is certain to gain paradise if he or she passes away before reaching puberty. Children are viewed as precious gifts from God and

need to be taken care of and protected by their parents and their surrounding communities. The primary way for children to attain spiritual development is to observe the personal spiritual practices of adults in their surrounding communities. Therefore, Islam not only gives these people the responsibility for the spiritual wellbeing of children, but also makes them accountable.[14]

Muslim youth work. In my studies and travels I have noticed that formal youth ministry as we understand it does not exist in Islamic majority countries. However, in the West, where Muslims are a tiny minority and the social structures of the old world have frayed (if not collapsed altogether), Muslims are making considerable effort to provide for the unique needs of those who have entered *bulugh* but have not yet attained *rush'd*.

There are 1,947 mosques in the United States, and of that number 350 of them (18%) have some kind of youth program or functioning youth ministry.[15] Muslim youth ministry has a regional and national infrastructure. For example, the Muslim Youth Association of North America has a paid national staff, which puts on national and regional training events for Muslim youth workers (paid and volunteer). They also facilitate events for Muslim young people. Leadership training is a huge priority in all Muslim youth work, and these events are analogous to Christian youth ministry events such as the National Youth Workers Convention by Youth Specialties and Simply Youth Ministry by Group. Though Muslim youth work bands and music have been slow to emerge on the US scene, they are now a normal feature of most gatherings.[16]

Mosque-based youth ministry usually has a program mix similar to Christian youth groups. *Teaching* is done in a variety of ways, either large group gatherings (such as in a mosque in Alexandria, Virginia, which hosts weekly "Pizza and Prophets" night, or in the "knowledge circle" small group approach taken by a mosque near Toronto). *Sports and recreation* is a normal feature in larger and more developed Muslim youth groups, such as the Islamic Society of Greater Lansing (Michigan), which offers sports leagues and tournaments. *Leadership development* is always a feature of regional and national Muslim youth work, but it also occurs at the local level, such as the Taric Youth Committee of a mosque in the Upper Midwest. *Service projects* round out the program of most well-developed youth ministries, such as the King Fahd Mosque of Culver City, California, which regularly does hospital visitation as well as senior center visitation. (We will look at Islamic youth ministry in much greater detail in chapter two.)

Hindu understanding of childhood and adolescence. The masses that populate the giant Indian subcontinent are in one sense a people steeped in tradition, and in another sense they are a people in social and cultural transition. The modern age has come to India, and with it a swelling middle class. The traditional extended family is a self-sufficient economic unit, with agriculture, fishing or crafts comprising its productive focus. In the extended family, roles and status are explicitly and securely demarcated by age, sex and kinship. Youth know their place, which is bound by this sticky web of relationships in the family and village. As a child grows she or he learns the skills necessary to function as an adult in the constellation of relationships that form the family and the village. There is no need for free association with other youths outside this small world, as even marriage is arranged on behalf of (but not necessarily for the benefit or pleasure of) the growing young person.

As Aileen Ross has pointed out, the emergence in India of the middle class, and the concomitant necessity of an educational infrastructure to prepare young people for work in the modern world, has brought about a nuclear family structure, which is supplanting the traditional structure. Where fathers and mothers are employed outside the home, the children go to school all day, and the backdrop is not the village but the city or suburb; "the father's authority tends to equalize with that of his wife, and children become more independent of parental control, and . . . agencies such as schools and youth organizations develop [which] impinge on the former total authority of parent over child."[17] In this context youth are not workers in the household economy but individuals preparing for their own freely chosen careers. This has become a big issue in India and even more so for the families of Indian background who have emigrated to Western countries.

Adherents of Hinduism, no matter where they live, believe in karma and reincarnation. This has profound implication for their view of children and adolescents; all children have spirituality *already within them* from their previous lives, and all that is required is to *awaken that spirituality as the children age.*[18]

One of the priorities of adult Hindus is to fulfill the obligations in this life to ensure they are making progress toward betterment in the next. Among these important and necessary duties is to help children and youth with their *dharma, karma* and *rina*. Dharma has to do with conscious spirituality; karma deals, in part, with sacred rituals that provide further connection to the gods and spiritual enlightenment; and rina is the notion of being responsible.[19]

Thus adults are obliged to help facilitate the emerging spirituality of their children and other youth.

Hindu youth work. As in all major religions in the United States, Hindu youth work is organized nationally, regionally and locally.

The Hindu Swayamsevak Sangh organization seeks to resource Hindu families with specific age-appropriate activities and spiritual events. It assumes that practicing Hindus in every community have found each other and are in mutually supportive relationships. Regarding Hindus in America, their website declares,

> The uniqueness of Hindu Dharma and the culture as practiced by the Hindu community has a significant contribution to make for the benefit of humanity. It is therefore essential for Hindus living in America to develop unity and harmony in their community to effectively promote these salient features. There are around two million Hindus in the US. Their contributions to the economic, social and cultural life are widely acclaimed.[20]

Chapters are found in every state.

Tattva, an online magazine for youth, was launched by the Swayamsevak Sangh organization and is a high-production spread with a variety of features of interest to Hindu high school and university age young people. *Tattva* means "essence" and, as such, tries to support the inner life and inner quest of Hindu youth as they learn about themselves and the Hindu religion.

There are two hundred Hindu temples in the United States. Most states have at least one. California has the highest number of temples, followed by New York, New Jersey and Texas.[21] Only a handful of temples have websites, but we can get a feel for temple-based Hindu youth ministry through the lens of the temple in Livermore, California. In 2001 this temple established a cultural center whose first mission is to promote Hindu religious education appropriate to children and youth. Subsequently, their programs have expanded to include music and dance, both of which are vital parts of worship in the temple.[22]

Buddhist understanding of childhood and adolescence. Buddhism is the predominant religion of Japan. Being a modern country and culture, there is a Japanese understanding and cultural stance toward youth and young people. It must be acknowledged, however, that Eastern religion is difficult to understand by those from the West or of monotheistic religions. Winston Davis acknowledges this difficulty and proposes a hermeneutical bridge that, once established, helps sociologists (and hopefully us) to understand religious affiliation, at least in the Buddhist framework.[23] Much of the religious activity or affiliation in Buddhism is instrumental in nature; that is, one goes to the shrine in order to achieve some good luck or fulfill a perceived obligation.[24] While "religion" is present, in no respects is it on the Buddhist mind as it is in Christianity or Islam.

Buddhists admire and acknowledge children not as individuals but as wonderful metaphors for a life of simplicity and spiritual essence.[25] As in Hinduism, Buddhism sees all life as part of a cycle, and thus children and youth have in-built spirituality that will eventually appear. The Four Noble Truths of Buddhism—(1) life as suffering, (2) suffering comes from craving what is impermanent, (3) suffering ceases through the extinction of craving, and (4) the path that keeps one from craving—can be understood intuitively by an individual as he or she matures. Programming specifically designed for young people is almost nonexistent within Buddhism. One researcher noted that in North America the children of Buddhist immigrants rarely remain Buddhist after they pass age eighteen. There seems to be no official concern about generation-to-generation transfer of Buddhism.[26]

Buddhist youth work. A rare exception to the lack of Buddhist concern for the religious education of youth can be seen at the Orange County Buddhist Church in Southern California. It gives every impression of being a temple on steroids when it comes to child, adolescent and family-centered programming, which is as extensive as any Protestant megachurch. From their website comes the invitation "From Ikebana, to the Digital Media Center—There are so many ways to get involved at OCBC. Take a look at what OCBC has to offer with our Social Groups, Cultural Groups, Sports Programs, Scouting and Youth Groups."[27]

From the root of Buddhism has sprung a new branch that takes a more intentional stance regarding young people. Soka Gakkai International, headquarted in Japan, is an international association of over seventy Soka Gakkai centers that aim to "realize the absolute happiness (enlightenment) of individuals and the prosperity of each country by the spreading understanding of the Buddhism of Nichiren. Toward that end, the SGI engages in various activities to promote peace, culture and education based on True Buddhism."[28] There are thirty-three Soka Gakkai centers in the United States, and all feature youth groups, Boy Scouts and Girl Scouts, and other youth-related programming. They also sponsor annual festivals and retreats. They have recently added full-time youth workers to their headquarters staff to increase their footprint in the United States among high school and university age young people.[29]

Jewish understanding of childhood and adolescence. Children are highly prized in Jewish religion, culture and tradition. To have children is a sign of God's blessing, and raising children is a high honor. In the words of Michael Shire,

> Childhood itself is an important state of being in Judaism, signified both by the cherished status of children in the classical literature and by the child-parent relationship that epitomizes the way in which the human-divine relationship is understood. Childhood is a symbolic depiction reflecting the special covenant between God and the People of Israel, which is characterized as a parent-child relationship.[30]

Within Judaism pre-adulthood is a time of learning to carry out the Ten Commandments and observing one's religious duty, both of which come into full play at age thirteen, the age of moral maturity, through the rite-of-passage bar mitzvah (for boys) or bat mitzvah (for girls). The rite is not like a commodity to be attained or something on a list to be checked off. Rather, it is something one *becomes* as well as something the community *bestows*.[31] The parents and the believing community are responsible to help a young person live into this reality.[32]

Jewish youth work. The B'nai B'rith Youth Association (BBYO) is one of many national Jewish organizations that seeks to engage middle school and high school Jewish young people. There are forty local offices throughout the United States. Their location depends on the Jewish population of the region. For example, Westchester Country, New York, just north of New York City, has an active program and extensive staff. By contrast, less-populated Arizona, Nevada and Utah have one BBYO.[33] Each region is divided into local chapters, which offer a range of meetings, programs and events.

For university students, the Jewish Student Association functions on all Ivy League campuses and most major universities nationwide. Harvard's JSA mission is "To serve as a resource to develop, inform, support, and enrich the Jewish community on campus. Our goals are to encourage student participation in Jewish events, build stronger ties among Jewish students and nearby Jewish organizations, and foster a sense of community."[34]

The BBYO and JSA are only two among many Jewish youth organizations. Others are local only or are based on conservative theology or practice. All are aimed at fostering "community," which is so vital in retaining and maintaining the Jewishness of its children.

Other religions' influence on Christian youth ministry. How does the youth ministry of other religions apply to Christian youth ministry? Not long ago religious "others" lived overseas. Unless North Americans lived in major metropolitan areas, they experienced people of other religions only through books and magazines like

National Geographic. Not so today. It is likely that students in our youth ministries will know someone from another religion. They may share a locker with a Muslim, sit next to a Buddhist in class or have a Hindu teammate.

And as our young people mature cognitively, they may wonder whether we Christians actually believe *their non-Christian friend is going to hell.* This should force us to be clear about our Christology, helping our young people know what we believe, why we believe and why it makes sense to believe what we do. In chapter seven we will look at helpful resources and how other youth workers approach this vital subject.

Here we will look at two other ways the rise of other religious youth ministries may be a good thing for Christian youth ministry. We will briefly look at the *marketplace* and *positive doubt* perspectives.

OTHER RELIGIONS' YOUTH MINISTRY AS COMPETITION FOR MARKET SHARE

While Christian youth ministry appears far more organized and developed, other religious traditions are catching up, finding their own young people responsive to the methods Christians use. In the North American context other religions are becoming increasingly aware that, unlike in their home countries, they exist in a free market of religious ideas and opportunities. They must compete or risk seeing their own youth converted by the sophisticated programs and techniques offered by Christian youth ministry. Seeing their own children as religious consumers, then, has forced these religions to become more adept at being religious producers. This "rational choice" vocabulary explains why especially Islam, Judaism and Hinduism have adopted the Christian approach to youth and youth ministry.[35]

From this perspective, given the market nature of free religious association among North American youth, as other religions improve their own youth ministry "products," Christian youth ministry must keep its competitive edge through innovation and improvement. For years Christian youth groups have happily accepted into their ranks youth of other faith traditions, and sometimes the parents of these youth have followed them into the church as well. There is no market law that precludes the reversal of this flow: other religions might leapfrog Christian youth ministry, resulting in the youth (and perhaps their parents) to begin flowing in the opposite direction.

In North American it seems that the vast majority of Jewish and Hindu youth ministries merely seek to conserve their own youth. The same is true of Buddhist youth work, what there is of it. Soka Gakkai, though, is much more *outreach* focused. As for Muslim youth work, about half of their youth group websites mention *dawa* events, which focus on outreach. A *dawa* event is not for the spiritual growth of Muslim young people but rather a venue for Muslim youth to bring their non-Muslim friends—an entry-level, no pressure "come and have fun with us and see that we're normal" opportunity. Does that sound familiar?

Most of us will not give this much thought until something like a megamosque is built down the street or next door to our own church. This very thing happened two years ago to a friend in New Jersey. The mosque next door has *two* full-time youth workers. They are showing up at the local high school sporting events, volunteering to help with drama club and offering their help to the PTA. In other words they are using all the tools Christian youth workers use to build bridges of influence with young people and their parents. My friend understands that on his high school campus the question no longer is how attractive a Baptist youth group is compared to the Assemblies or Presbyterian youth groups. *The playing field has changed dramatically.* Now Christian youth ministry is compared to Muslim youth ministry!

THE POSITIVE DOUBT PERSPECTIVE

While most of our students will not have to choose between their youth group and going to "Pizza and Prophets" with their friend Rashid, they may experience doubt about Jesus as the *only* way as they are repeatedly confronted with the new cultural norm of tolerance or the repugnant thought of their volleyball team member facing eternity in hell simply because he or she was born into a Hindu family.

Cognitive development, what I call the cerebral upgrade (see chap. 7), commonly includes a revisiting of things once held true. That new mental power, due to the completed wiring of the prefrontal cortex, makes all things new to the person. Picture being in a room with no doors or windows (the childhood brain). Then (as the cerebral upgrade happens), boom, there's a window! Three weeks later there's another one! And what's that? It's a door! These new portals to the outside world invite exploration.

I counsel parents, when their son or daughter expresses doubt about God or something important, that their heart response should be "Thank God!" This young brain is getting upgraded, which is how God created this brain to function.

Awareness of other religions is like a new window or door that was not previously there. These things call into question previously held assumptions. This is an important and necessary step in the spiritual formation of our youth.

When I do small group processing of issues related to God and faith, I often ask my college freshmen Intro to Youth Ministry students, "At what point did your faith become your own? That is, do you see your Christian faith as a carryover of what your parents told you, or has there come a point when you realized it is now your faith, not theirs? Be honest. Tell me your story."

Their answers are very interesting. Most have to do with suffering or externally triggered doubt. Suffering fosters the question, Can a good God be that mean or uncaring? Tolerance training at school or the awareness of good people who are religious "others" can foster the response, *Yikes, does what I believe make any sense in the real world?*

I want my youth group students to know and understand that other teenagers their age who are Muslim and Hindus are very happy with their faith, just like we are. This forces the construction of a new window or door in their cognitive room.

To really get a feel for what is happening when it comes to the youth ministry of other religions, let's take a close look at Islam.

THE SCOPE AND NATURE OF MUSLIM YOUTH WORK

Have They All Read
Purpose-Driven Youth Ministry?

The day is coming, and has likely already come in some places, that a student in your youth ministry will come home from high school and a conversation like this will take place:

> MOM. Hi, Jenn, how was your day?
>
> JENN. It was great, we've got a new assistant coach for the girls volleyball team, her name is Rashida, and she's really nice!

And Rashida, a full-time youth worker at the local mosque, has volunteered her time and expertise at the school. She seeks to do relational youth ministry, just like the thousands of Young Life, Youth for Christ and church-based youth pastors who give their time to volunteering in sports, drama, music and other venues.[1]

In chapter one I spoke briefly about student ministry from the standpoint of several religions, including Islam. Here is a full account of my research on the foundations and models of Muslim youth ministry. In the coming decades Islam will be the most visible of the "religious others" in our communities. My research encompassed the United States, Canada and the United Kingdom.

Here I attempt to locate Muslim youth work in a historical and sociological framework. I give an account of how this research was conducted, as any serious research effort should. After summarizing the parameters of Muslim youth ministry's footprint nationally, regionally and locally, I describe how this youth work is anchored theologically in the Qur'an and hadiths (the reported sayings and activities of Muhammad not contained in the Qur'an), as well as culturally in the Arabic words associated with adolescents and youth. I close this section with an overview of Muslim youth ministry praxis. Christian youth workers will readily recognize key features of Christian youth ministry replicated by their Muslim counterparts.

This research has, among many things, a particular microlevel value. When a large mosque is built in your neighborhood and you see from the mosque website that they have youth programs, you will understand how their youth workers see themselves and what they are doing. This knowledge will be a good first step before building a bridge of friendship and possible joint Christian-Muslim youth group service projects.

INTRODUCTION

Though Islam has been a global religion since the Middle Ages, it has come to the forefront of attention in the West through highly visible negative events. Though each of these events cast Islam in a less than positive light, thinking people understand that Islam is not a monolithic religion bent on jihad. Rather, Islam comes in many versions, similar to Christianity and Judaism.

Scholars have shed light on the various contours of Islam in many ways, especially juxtaposed with other religious faiths. Examples include Christine Carabain and Rene Bekker's 2012 study comparing philanthropic behavior of Christians, Muslims and Hindus in the Netherlands. Khari Brown and Ronald E. Brown's 2011 examination of interfaith contact in America. And the intersections of Christianity and Islam in Britain by Steve Bell and Colin Chapman.[2]

It should come as no surprise that Muslim parents care about their own children and their religious faith development. This is particularly true for families who emigrate from a Muslim majority nation to a Western nation where the Muslim population is a tiny percentage of the whole.[3] It is also no surprise that some Muslim leaders in Western countries are concerned that there may be a weakening of the faith (if not outright faith abandonment) among children and youth born to first-generation immigrant Muslim parents now raising their children a culture awash with mores completely foreign to traditional Islam.[4]

This research explores an important outgrowth of this Muslim concern for their own young people: Muslim youth work. Here we will explore the Qur'anic, philosophical and sociocultural foundations of Muslim youth work, as well as Muslim youth work praxis.

THEORETICAL AND RESEARCH ANTECEDENTS

Subculture identity theory. Subculture identity theory, a subfield within sociology of religion, provides a conceptual home for the consideration of Muslim youth work. It provides the theoretical framework to analyze the processes by which religions and religious groups maintain (and grow) within modern, pluralistic societies. This maintenance and growth occurs by creating a subculture that affirms, according to Christian Smith, collective identities that provide adherents with meaning and belonging.[5] Smith explains, "In a pluralistic society, religious groups which are better at transmitting and employing the cultural tools needed to create both clear distinction from, and significant engagement and tension with other relevant out groups, will be relatively successful."[6] We will see some of these "cultural tools" when Muslim youth work praxis is considered.

Subcultural identity theory is a new field first given impetus in the United States through the study of religious denominations, and particularly those labeled "evangelical." Subculture identity theory forms the backdrop of studies regarding Muslim youth as well. For example, young people in Germany of Turkish descent whose parents are essentially secular are flocking to a "pop" version of Islam in which the rediscovery of Islam is seen as "young, chic, and cool."[7]

Attachment theory. Another conceptual home for the consideration of Muslim youth work stems from attachment theory. Here the strength of personal bonds and connections (with parents, significant other adults and like-minded peers) is seen as not only important for emotional health and flourishing, but also plays a part in the transmission of culture (including religion) from one generation to the next.[8] Academic studies of attachment and religion abound, as well as specific studies that demonstrate a causal connection between attachment and youth religiosity.[9] Furthermore, researchers are beginning to explore attachment theory and Muslim youth religiosity. For example, a study of 1,861 youth of Turkish and Moroccan descent living in the Netherlands showed a weakening of religious identity within the second generation.[10] Another study posits that attachment has a great deal to do with religious conversion.[11] This is very relevant not only for the relationship of the Muslim youth leader to individual youth but the relationship of Muslim youth and Muslim youth workers to non-Muslims as various *dawa* (outreach/evangelism) programs become part of the youth group's schedule.

We will see examples of attachment theory in practice (latently if not explicitly) by Muslim youth workers in both North America and Europe when we consider Muslim youth work praxis.

Youth religiosity research. After hundreds of studies across the globe, the significant connection of youth religiosity and prosocial behavior is incontrovertibly established in the social sciences. While religious youth work (no matter what the religion) may be good for theological and missional reasons, social scientists are interested in youth religiosity from the standpoint of a civil society. Higher youth religiosity, compared to less religious peers, means (among many other things) better emotional and physical health, improved relationships with parents, better academic performance, clearer sense of purpose, and a greater willingness to give time and money to help others. High religiosity also means less alcohol and drug use, less sexual activity, and less criminality.[12]

While initial youth religiosity research primarily focused on the Christian faith, Muslim youth religiosity research is beginning to appear, either in comparison with other religions or with Muslim youth as the sole research focus. A representative comparative-religion study is the work of David Dollahite, who explored the likelihood of Christian and Muslim youth in the United States to forgo risky (and sinful) behaviors for the sake of a higher good and higher benefit.[13] Mark Grey authored another important study in which Muslim young people were the sole focus of religiosity and personality development.[14]

Insofar as a common component of youth religiosity research is participation in a religious youth group, the study of Muslim youth groups and Muslim youth work is both relevant and contributory to this research.

DATA AND METHODS

Personal interviews. After reviewing Muslim and Muslim youth work websites in both North America and the United Kingdom, I sought to interview key Muslim youth work trainers. Some websites did not have updated contact information. Other Muslim leaders or their organizational office personnel did not answer emails or phone calls. However, I was able to have long phone conversations with Muslim youth work leaders from Vancouver, Toronto and Chicago. On a sabbatical trip to the United Kingdom in February 2012, I was able to have face-to-face interviews with key Muslim youth leaders who comprise, in my opinion, the brain trust of Muslim youth work. The three resided in Oxford, Bradford and Nottingham.

While it was no small task to find and gain access to these six leaders, succinctly convey the macro- and micropurpose of my research, and seek to gain trust and credibility in the crucial first sixty seconds of contact, once I was "in" the conversations held were lengthy and rich in two-way discovery. I came away from the experience with a deep respect for the heart these men had for young people and the work of youth ministry.

Source documents. Especially in the United Kingdom there are rich resources for the scholarly consideration of the foundational understandings that Muslim youth work rests on. Additionally, there are resources that discuss youth work and the merits or appropriateness of various youth work models. These resources will be discussed and cited subsequently in this chapter.

Web research. I stumbled across, as is sometimes the case in searching the Web, a fascinating and comprehensive site. Salatomatic .com touts itself as the "World's most comprehensive guide to mosques and Islamic schools." Of interest here, though tangential to the research focus of this chapter, is that this site allows persons to write reviews of individual mosques and rate them on a scale of one to five, a bit like TripAdvisor.com or Hotels.com. In some cases one can know from these reviews the proximity of public transportation or if the restrooms are clean!

There are mosque-related news stories on salatomatic.com as well. For example, the June 21, 2012, homepage featured stories that included the Islamic Center of Murfreesboro (Tennessee) (rated 5.0 by reviewers) and touting their tornado and flood-relief efforts locally, and their ongoing Haiti relief work. A Turkish mosque and their new building program is also featured. When construction is finished, women will be able to pray at the same time as men. (As is normal in Islam, men and women gather separately.) There is a featured story of a mosque "going green" in Abu Dhabi. And the first underwater mosque is under construction in Saudi Arabia!

Of direct interest to the study of Muslim youth work is the searchable feature of the website. For every continent on the globe one can search by country, by region/state/province and by city. Information includes a list of mosques and their "denomination" (e.g., Shia, Sunni or Sufi). Information on each mosque is as comprehensive as possible. If there is any kind of youth group, school or "Sunday school," it is listed under "Services Offered." If this youth group has a website, the URL given. This makes possible the collection of quantitative data. From January 2011 to April 2012 two Nyack College students and I examined the salatomatic.com information on over three thousand mosques.[15] Among those mosques, if a youth group website was given, we studied it as well.

THE BIG PICTURE OF MUSLIM YOUTH WORK

Mosque based. How prevalent is mosque-based youth work in the countries studied? (We will look again at mosque-based youth work when Muslim youth work praxis is considered.)

While the majority of mosques do not yet have their own youth groups, in the United States, Canada and the United Kingdom there are regionally based youth ministries that seek to provide Muslim youth work infrastructure. These would be especially helpful for smaller mosques that do not have the personnel, vision, or resources to provide their own youth programming.

Regionally based. Regionally based Muslim youth work takes on a variety of forms. Houston, Texas, for example, has a regional youth center with several program options including service projects, a soccer league, karate classes, and open volleyball and basketball nights. They use three words to describe their misson: activism, spirituality and *tarbiya* (the latter meaning "education or increased knowledge").[16]

Another example of regional Muslim youth work is the Muslim Youth Camp of California. Held annually since 1962, MYC offers a one-week premier camping experience. Their mission statement gives the heart of the organization's purpose:

> The Muslim Youth Camp brings Muslim families and individuals of diverse backgrounds together for a fun-filled week of Islamic living, learning and inspirational experiences in nature. By encouraging camaraderie, personal spiritual exploration and respect for diversity of Islamic practice, MYC seeks to be a strong catalyst in the creation of American Muslim identities.[17]

A typical day at MYC involves daily prayers, swimming and group sports, teamwork competition, classes, campfire and free time. Their marketing materials indicate they not only draw from the state of California but nationally and internationally.

Regional Muslim youth work organizations often provide the leadership training infrastructure to support Muslim youth work in other regions or in local mosques. The youth department of the British Columbia Muslim Association has a full-time paid director whose office and volunteers offer multiple services:

- formulate guidelines and policies for youth group at each branch or chapter for common good

- develop a program of events and activities with focus on Islamic values and leadership training
- conduct yearly Muslim youth conventions
- sports and recreation services to promote sports activities.[18]

As in Canada and the United States there are multiple Muslim youth work organizations in the United Kingdom that are local (but not mosque based) and have a regional draw. They function akin to parachurch organizations so common in Christianity. One of the most developed of these organizations is Muslim Youth Skills, headquartered in Bradford. They offer youth work training courses. The current list of courses offered includes

- Engaging Young People
- Understanding Culture
- Islam and Muslims
- Introduction to Muslim Youth Work
- Tackling Crime[19]

Muslim Youth Skills also offers onsite consultation by their trained leaders as well as personal counseling and youth-work-related problem solving. They position themselves as offering "first class service to the Public, Private, and Third Sectors." And they declare,

> Muslim Youth Skills draws upon over a decade of experience in the youth and community work field. Our trainers and consultants come form various professions, thus enriching the services that we offer. Although our services combine an understanding of religious, cultural and spiritual needs of Muslims specifically, our service is not exclusive to this community. Many of our programmes and workshops respond to wider social issues.[20]

As we have seen Muslim youth work exists at the local and regional level. There are many national-level organizations facilitating Muslim youth work as well.

Nationally based. The Muslim Association of Canadian Youth is a department within the Muslim Association of Canada and exists to provide activities that reflect the values of faith, brotherhood, personal development, citizenship, inclusiveness, relevance and excellence. They also publish a monthly magazine titled *My Voice.*[21]

In the United States a representative example is Muslim Youth of North America: "Connect, Inspire, Belong." A national gathering related to Ramadan was held in July 2012. Other activities include an annual convention, summer camps and resources for Muslim parents.[22] Another project is sponsored by the Muslim American Society. The Muslim Youth Leadership Forum: Building Young Muslims for a Better America states its goal as

> to mentor and prepare young Muslim leaders to provide leadership not only to the Muslim community but the greater American society at large. The institutional design focuses on developing and enhancing leadership skill sets of Muslim youth that will impact America's civic, social, economic and religious life. Youth participants will be placed in a leadership social mentoring network that will allow them to communicate after the initial forum on an ongoing basis with qualified mentors and other forum participants.[23]

In the United States books written for young people to affirm and support their Muslim religious faith are beginning to appear. The subculture identity theorists would understand the publication of magazines and books as contributing toward the creation of an understandable and acceptable Muslim youth framework to see themselves in their religion.

The United Kingdom is rich with organizations seeking to service the needs of British Muslim young people. These include Young Muslims UK (ymuk.net), and Muslim Youth Skills (muslimyouthskills.co.uk). One of most developed organizations is the Muslim Youthwork Foundation, whose mission is "Creating safe spaces for Muslim young people to explore personal, social, spiritual, and political choices."[24] Their website offers (among many other choices) a poets' corner, mentoring opportunities, Muslim youth-related art and a create-your-own video feature called "Witness." The MYWF has a subsidiary website, muslim youth.net, which is "the coolest online space for Muslim youth!"

QUR'ANIC, HADITHIC AND CULTURAL FOUNDATIONS

Christian youth ministry thinkers, as well as practitioners prone to reflection, seek to anchor what they do in the Bible, Christian theology and cultural theory. Recent works by Kenda Dean and Andrew Root, Pete Ward, and Tony Jones are representative examples.[25] Muslim youth workers are beginning to similarly reflect on their work.

When asked for a basis of Muslim youth work in the Qur'an, many Muslim youth leaders will, without hesitation, speak of sura 18, "The Cave." Here we see the Prophet taking seriously the spirituality and spiritual potential of young men:

> [Prophet], we shall tell you their story as it really was. They were young men who believed in their Lord, and we gave them more guidance. We gave strength to their hearts when they stood up and said, "Our Lord is the Lord of heavens and earth. We shall never call upon any god other than Him." (sura 18:13-14)

In the verses surrounding this text we see that the belief of these young men was considered a sign by the Prophet. We also see them as capable of not only belief but of following the way and being divinely guided.

In Islamic culture puberty is the mark of entry to accountability and responsibility in life. The Arabic word is *taklif*, legal obligation. It is incumbent on Muslim parents (and now youth workers as well) to help young people "get it," that is, to believe and behave in such a way as to reflect they are in the Way (called *Deen* in Arabic). Verses in the Qur'an such as sura 41:44—"a guide and a healing to those who believe"—applies to not just adults but young people as well.[26] Similarly, exhortations to justice (sura 4:35) and to be a receiver and giver of mercy (sura 1:1) apply to all Muslims who are of age.

Yet another foundation of Muslim youth work comes out of the Arabic language and culture, the concept of *ilm*, which simply means "knowledge" or "knowledge of."[27] Allah is seen as the source of truth and knowledge, and it is the responsibility of all Muslims to know and follow this truth. Those who do not yet know this truth must be taught it by those who do. Whatever the sphere of Muslim youth work, be it local, regional or national, there is tremendous emphasis in Islam to teach this knowledge or to teach those who will teach. Teaching, in many mosques, is *everything*.

While *ilm* has to do with what the individual *knows*, *ummah* has to do with what the individual *feels*. Muslims are to feel connected to other Muslims around the globe in a sense of unity in their faith.[28] With Muslims living not only in "Muslim" nations but scattered abroad, the meaning of *ummah* has been much discussed in the Muslim community.[29] Nevertheless, for those who provide the youth infrastructure *ummah* provides a conceptual foundation for the websites, events and gatherings of Muslim young people locally, regionally and nationally. Muslim youth work helps youth feel connected to a larger whole.

Among Muslim youth workers there are multiple tensions as to what constitutes acceptable youth ministry practice. These tensions usually relate to cultural practice and tradition. For example, I asked the six Muslim youth work leaders I interviewed about the use of music in youth work. All of them stated that music must glorify Allah, which is theoretically possible. But they would *never* use music in a youth gathering at any level—mosque, region or national gathering. It would be too controversial. These leaders are concerned with helping, preserving and conserving the good character of Muslim young people as they maneuver within a culture awash in non-Muslim values. One Muslim youth worker, citing sura 68:4 of the Qur'an—"indeed, your character is of a vast ethos"—stated, "I have [a concern] of many current models, which appear to be based on and regulated by the norms of consumer society."[30]

Based on the Qur'an and the hadiths we can establish a threefold purpose for all Muslims, including young ones who have attained *taklif*, as (1) attain faith, (2) do good works, and (3) be one who is God conscious or God fearing.[31]

Let's examine how Muslim youth work seeks to do this.

MODELS OF MUSLIM YOUTH WORK PRAXIS

Nonconfessional models. Especially in the United Kingdom, much of Muslim youth work is essentially secular; that is, it is done by men and women (who happen to be Muslims) who desire to help young people who are economically hurting, feeling disenfranchised by the larger culture and are seen as "at risk."[32]

With 33 percent of Britain's' Muslim population under the age seventeen, and 71 percent under the age thirty-one, social scientists and civil authorities were becoming alarmed that many of these young people live in impoverished swaths of the city, which breeds despair, crime and radicalization.[33]

Scholarly interest in this subpopulation of the United Kingdom has been robust, and the future of these disenfranchised youth has been a concern even prior to the terrorist bombings at London's King's Cross Station on July 7, 2007.[34]

In "community youth work" youth workers engage young people in recreation and positive interaction. In the United Kingdom nearly four thousand full-time community youth workers are employed, many of whom are Muslim.[35]

One-on-one or small group discussions may take place on issues such as citizenship, bullying, discrimination, sexuality, drug abuse and identity, which are relevant to young people in most communities. Additionally, such nonconfessional youth work may include sports programs like football, basketball and table tennis.[36]

A very creative approach targeting the personal needs of Muslim young people is the Muslim Youth Helpline. Established in 2001 MYH is led by trained mental health professionals who train the volunteers who receive the phone calls, staff the live online chat service and respond to email inquiries.[37] Muslim Youth Helpline is an example of secular Muslim youth work that helps young people explore what it means to be Muslim in a Western nation.

Secular Muslim youth work in the United Kingdom comes from a *deficit* perspective.[38] That is, the focus is on the felt needs, the problems and issues faced in the daily life of Muslim young people. These needs might be emotional, safety related or the need for hope to function in a culture in which they feel misunderstood or not welcome.

In North America various mosques and Islamic centers offer a variety of programs parallel to secular youth organizations, but the *deficit* perspective is virtually nonexistent. The flavor of nonconfessional Muslim youth work in North America seems more focused on *enrichment*, not deficit. For example, Muslim Boy Scouts and Girl Scouts are widespread in North America.[39] Muslim Scouts engage, train and empower parents as troop leaders, so the effort becomes a family activity. (It is, however, sex-segregated.)

North American Muslims also have the equivalent to Big Brothers Big Sisters. The Muslim Family Network of Calgary explains its program:

> The Big Sister/Big Brother program has been developed so that children can experience the richness, excitement, and warmth of an Islamic environment, a place where children learn the importance of caring, sharing, tolerance, patience, and working with others.
>
> In addition to arts and crafts, recreational and outdoor activities (including field trips), the program will offer Islamic activities based on weekly themes.
>
> The classes also provide the opportunity for university and high school students to gain important skills while they serve as assistants and volunteers for the program. Each week of the program will include activities and learning based on a theme.[40]

While not strictly secular, the BC Muslims organization in British Columbia, Canada, markets a national resource called the Ayal Muslim Youth Help Line to help young people with personal problems. They affirm that all their phone counselors have been raised in Canada and are practicing Muslims.[41]

Confessional models. Explicitly religious Muslim youth work models encompass most mosque-based and regional and national Muslim youth organizations youth work. While most of these organizations include topics and services germane to young people of any religion—sports and leadership development, service opportunities and evangelism. The chief purpose of all Muslim youth programming is to help youth become comfortable and confident in their Muslim beliefs. The Muslim equivalent to evangelism or outreach is the Arabic word *Dawa*, which means "invitation." *Dawa* events are explicitly planned so Muslim youth can invite their non-Muslim friends. Not unlike Christian youth groups, the program mix varies from mosque to mosque. The following is a sample of the youth ministries of specific mosques.

Table 2.1. Mosques and Mosque-Based Youth Work in Selected Countries, 2011–2012

	Number of mosques	Youth groups (number and percent)	Main province/ state/region	Number and percent of mosques in this area
Canada	347	80 (23%)	Ontario	208 (27%)
United States	1947	350 (18%)	California	302 (18%)
UK	1131	328 (29%)*	Yorkshire & Humber*	239 (21%)
Netherlands	33	6 (18%)		
Norway	4	2 (50%)		
Switzerland	12	6 (50%)		

*This count of youth groups does not include the 302 mosques in London, which were not studied.

Teaching. In a very conservative mosque teaching would include the memorization of key passages of the Qur'an and more wide-ranging discussions of the implications of Islamic teaching for everyday life. The mosque at 1 Beech Road in Luton, England, offers regular Qur'an classes for boys and girls. The mosque in Alexandria, Virginia, offers a regular "Pizza and Prophets" night, which includes good food and good study and discussion of the Qur'an or hadiths. The youth group at a megamosque in the Los Angeles area offers a ninety-minute Sunday school class that includes an hour-long lecture followed by discussion. The high school group of the large Waterloo Mosque outside of Toronto has a very active youth program that includes small groups for processing that day's or the week's teaching. Called "knowledge circles" these help young people feel part of "Generation M," that is, Generation Muslim.

The Mordern Islamic Center in Surrey, England, calls their youth program "Friday Circles." A typical Friday program involves a brief time of teaching (called "Islamic Reminders"), quiz competition, puzzles, projects and food.

Sports and recreation. Regional and mosque-based Muslim youth work typically involves sports and recreation. The Islamic Society of Greater Lansing (Michigan) offers a Spring Break Challenge that includes basketball, soccer and football. Similarly, the Young Muslims of the Teaneck, New Jersey, mosque offers a three-on-three basketball tournament for different age groups. A mosque in Bern, Switzerland, offers a series of two-day summer day-camp programs for children and youth. Recreation and sports are the main ingredients, but there are designated times to inspire and support these young people spiritually. In Saskatoon, Saskatchewan, the boys-only sports program (basketball and volleyball) takes place on Wednesday and Saturday nights. The London (Ontario) Muslim Mosque offers drop-in basketball for boys on Friday nights and karate classes on Saturday nights. The Aisha Mosque in Birmingham, England, has sports night every Saturday night for their youth program called "United Kingdom Islamic Mission Youth."

Leadership training. Leadership training is a recurrent theme in Muslim confessional youth work. For example, the Yaseen Foundation in the San Francisco Bay Area has an age-divided (13-14, 15-18) youth club led by an elected group of young people under the advisement of former members who are in their early twenties. Similarly, the Husaini Youth Group in Peterborough, England, has a large number of young people on their leadership committee. The Taric Islamic Centre in Toronto seeks to develop leadership in young people by their participation the Taric Youth Committee, which teaches leadership and teamwork skills.

Service projects. Not unlike Christian youth groups, the King Fahd Mosque of Culver City, California, youth group makes monthly visits to the local hospital and senior citizens center. This mosque has significant resources devoted to youth work, with a youth center that has weekly hangout programs called "The Spiritual Spot." Their youth group meets here prior to these monthly service outings and uses the center as a base for planning future service efforts. The regionally based Muslim Association of Arizona helps Muslim young people get involved in community services projects such as graffiti cleanup, distributing food at shelters, blood drives and toy drives. The Islamic Association of Saskatoon Regina Mosque includes an orphan sponsorship program aimed at helping young people (and their parents) support poor Muslim children in Palestine, Pakistan, Sudan and Kosovo.

Dawa. This word comes up frequently in the content of regional and mosque-based Muslim youth websites. A good example is the mosque Es Salam in Chandler, Arizona. They have recently completed their youth center (6,500 sq. ft.) and have plans to add a much larger facility that will include indoor swimming pools, sports courts, and additional office and meeting space for counseling and classes. The Kingston-Upon Thames (Surrey) club and sports programs include the goal of servicing the entire community. Young people are welcome at their activities, without regard to religion. This welcome is mirrored by the Epson and Ewell Islamic Society (Surrey) in their full calendar of youth activities, including frequent trips to the paintball facility.

CONCLUSIONS

In this chapter I have presented some of the key religious and cultural foundations of Muslim youth work. We have seen that Muslim youth work not only rests on applying relevant Qur'anic texts but also an Islamic understanding of adolescence. Table 2.1 provides a count of Muslim youth groups and their country or region. Future research will establish how these youth groups have changed over time.

While many British Muslim youth ministries are based on the *deficit model*, which means they address critical problems related to being British and Muslim, North America Muslim youth ministries are more often based on an *enrichment* model. This distinction and its implications certainly deserve further study.

The study of Muslim youth work rests comfortably in at least three bases of social science inquiry. First, *subculture identity theory* helps us understand what is happening as Muslims seek to facilitate youth work and youth groups for their own sons and daughters. These youth groups provide a place where being Muslim is affirmed, strengthened and celebrated. Second, *attachment theory* helps conceptualize what happens in Muslim youth groups, youth camps and youth conferences in terms of peer bonding, which is especially important for young people whose neighborhood or school is not majority Muslim. Third, *youth religiosity research* analyzes how young Muslims experience and live out their faith, how youth work contributes to this religiosity, and the life outcomes of this faith.

THE RISE OF SYNCRETISTS AND NONES

Understanding Those Whose
Faith Is to Have None at All
or, More Tolerantly, Believe
That All Faiths Are Equal

In my decades of student ministry I have rarely met an atheistic teenager who is evangelistic, that is, one who is missional in his or her desire to convert peers from faith to nonfaith. Typically such an adolescent is raised in a home with no living spirituality. Religious faith is not seen as important or relevant; there are more pressing and tangible concerns. The National Study of Youth and Religion (NSYR) observes that young people turn out a lot like their parents in many ways, including faith or lack thereof (see table 3.1). Therefore, when thinking about nones we need to include their parents and family context.

The study of declining religious participation and belief among adults in the United States is a fertile field for social science. The American Religious Identification Survey of 2008 revealed that the number of adults identifying themselves as having no religion increased from 13.1 million in 1990 to 30.4 million—15 percent of the population—in 2008. Among Americans ages eighteen to twenty-nine the figure is 22 percent. The ARIS study also revealed that the majority of nones are "neither atheists nor theists but rather agnostics and deists (59%) and perhaps best described as skeptics."[1] This observation is important when considering parent-student ministry implications later in this chapter.

Table 3.1. Parents' Faith and Their Teens' Faith

Parent importance of faith	Teen importance of faith				
	Extremely	Very	Somewhat	Not very	Not at all
extremely important	30%	37%	24%	5%	3%
very important	14%	32%	36%	12%	5%
fairly important	7%	23%	38%	21%	10%
somewhat important	8%	15%	41%	20%	16%
not very important	3%	11%	37%	22%	26%
not important at all	2%	15%	37%	19%	28%

Source: Christian Smith and Melinda Denton, *Soul Searching* (New York: Oxford University Press, 2005), p. 56.

As we think more specifically about youth and emerging adults and the subject of nones, the NSYR is a good place to begin. Only about 20 percent of emerging adults are engaged in their Christian faith, pray, read the Bible and are active in their church or parachurch organization. This is about a 10 percent decline from those same young people five years previous.

Interestingly, this 20 percent figure of active faith and engagement for nineteen- to twenty-five-year-olds has not changed in forty years, according to the General Social Survey.[2] In a helpful step to understanding the other 80 percent, the NSYR five-year follow-up among individuals now ages nineteen to twenty-four divided emerging adults into six major religious types, three of which would fit under the none umbrella.[3]

"Religiously indifferent" nineteen- to twenty-four-year-olds (25% of this age cohort) don't oppose religious faith; they simply see no need for it their lives right now. Religion may be wonderful for others, and they are certainly tolerant of religious people, but faith is not a priority for them. Smith and Snell, after interviewing a large portion of their sample population, posit a possible "cognitive logic" of the religiously indifferent:

> Major premise: Serious religion means no partying and no sex before marriage.
>
> Minor premise: I do or may want to party and have sex before marriage.
>
> Conclusion: I am not legitimately part of or interested in serious religion.[4]

The second category is "religiously disconnected" emerging adults (5% of this age cohort). They have no real knowledge of religious faith; it was not part of their family's DNA. They do not favor or oppose religious faith; it's just a nonissue to them.

The third category, "irreligious" nineteen- to twenty-four-year-olds (10% of this age cohort) are skeptical of religious faith and are able to articulate, with some incredulousness, their reasons for nonbelief. Irreligious emerging adults usually have parents who were either once religious but left their faith, or who were agnostic or atheistic from the outset.

ANTECEDENTS OF NONENESS

Family context. We have already seen that adolescents and emerging adults tend to mimic the religiosity of their parents. It makes perfect sense that a child growing up in a family context devoid of God talk or even Easter and Christmas church attendance, and being educated in a school system that steers clear of any mention of faith, would quite naturally be irreligious. The NSYR is only one of many empirical studies that affirm the parent religiosity and teenage/young adult religiosity link.[5] As a youth worker these are my favorite not-yet-Christian people. They may know nothing about faith and may not be interested, but at least they are not hostile. (I love helping these youths and their parents gradually come to the realization that perhaps they should think about faith.)

The behavior context. Does belief create behavior or does behavior create belief? Social scientists love to study things like this.[6] In short, the academic consensus is that it goes both ways. This connects well to the "cognitive logic" in which an individual wants to be free to party and have sex and therefore steers clear of religious belief, expression or close relationships with those who seem to have an active faith. Here the individual sees religious faith as a straightjacket to be avoided, that religious faith is regressive and limiting to personal freedom. I have known many adolescents who held this view. Religious faith would, they believe, spoil their fun.

The intellectual context. Among the main reasons adolescents and emerging adults step away from an active faith and become, for all practical purposes, nones is that they cannot reconcile faith and science. Other intellectual reasons for faith exit include rejection of the exclusive claims of Christianity and the perception that the church is hostile to doubt. Additionally, some none young people see the church's answer to many issues, sexuality, for example, as simplistic and judgmental.[7]

The negative experience context. Many of us who work with youth and young adults know young people who have been deeply scarred. It is extremely difficult, for example, for someone raised by a judgmental, vindictive and abusive parent (even one who was outwardly religious) to sense God's love or a desire to affiliate with a church.[8] Aside from faith-killing negative experiences in the home, there are ample additional sources of emotional toxicity that foster distance from faith. Among these are clergy child abuse, made famous in the 1990s and 2000s in the Roman Catholic Church, and the departure of a much-loved youth pastor. Breaking these important relational bonds can trigger an exit from a youth group and the church. Certainly, experiencing hypocrisy in the church also serves as a faith repellant to young people. Left unchecked, negative experiences foster cynicism, which is certainly inimical to faith.

THE EMERGING CULTURAL INFRASTRUCTURE FOR NONENESS

No matter how a person becomes a none, there is a growing multifaceted movement in the United States (and Western Europe) that affirms, encourages and supports individuals in their nonaffiliation with religious faith. It is important for those of us in Christian youth ministry to be aware of this movement.

Among the most developed none organizations is Recovering from Religion, which likes to highlight Mark Twain's famous words: "Faith is believing what you know ain't so."[9] They introduce themselves with the words:

> If you are one of the many people who have determined that religion no longer has a place in their life, but are dealing with the after-effects in some way or another, Recovering From Religion (RR) may be just the right spot for you. We welcome everyone, from doubting theist to ardent atheist, and our goal is to assist you in dealing with the negative impact of religion in your life. We are honored to be part of your journey to be free from faith![10]

The organization has no youth outreach, but they have support groups across North America (and globally). Undoubtedly the subject of parenting teenagers in nonfaith is raised in such gatherings.

Another example is the Reason Rally Coalition, which held its first major gathering in Washington, D.C., in 2012, with twenty thousand in attendance. It was billed as a celebration of secular values and the nontheist view of the world. Among the twenty sponsors of the co-alition is the Secular Student Alliance.[11] Unlike other none organizations, the Secular Student Alliance is specifically for university and high school students. The alliance offers resources to begin, maintain and grow Secular Student Alliance groups on school campuses, and there are over four hundred of these groups in America.[12] Beyond none organizations and events, there are emerging social networks for nones, such as facebook.com/skeptictalk as well as books that affirm and celebrate nonbelief. Titles include *Happily Godless: A Young Adult's Guide to Atheism* by Paul Donvan, and *The Phoenix and the Peacock: A Tale of Feathers and Hidden Treasure* by Sienna Storm.[13] The websites and literature of the none organizations reveal that there is immense optimism that secularism will continue to gain in visibility and influence.

SYNCRETISM

Every fall a very strange thing happens in the United Kingdom. If one happens to be on a flight into or out of any of London's four airports just after sunrise or just before sunset, Roman cities appear outlined in some of the fields below. I am not kidding. I read about this phe-nomenon twenty years ago and have seen it with my own eyes once. Since one of my odd interests is Roman Britain, I nearly yelped with glee at the sight.

While the phenomenon seems mysterious, it really is anything but. Just below the plowed surface of many fields in the United Kingdom lie the stone foundations of Roman buildings. The prox-imity of these stones to the surface has an impact on moisture re-tention, which affects the growth rate of the crops directly above. Thin-soil crops grow slower than crops growing in deeper soil. Late in the growing season this growth differential is noticeable from the air, and especially when the sun is at low angle. The sun's low angle throws into relief the crop growth differentials, and thus Roman streets, houses, shops, government and military buildings are all of a sudden *there*.

In this chapter I throw into relief an aspect of youth and emerging adult belief about religion: many have a faith whose constituent parts seem to have been chosen à la carte. We will come at this from several angles: quantitative research, sociological-cultural theory and theological reflection. Each in turn will throw into relief in a slightly different way the syncretistic nature of adolescent faith today.

Quantitative research. When seen from the angle of social science research, which involves surveys and statistics, a decades-long shift in religious allegiances in the United States is thrown into relief. In the 1960s and 1970s as the precipitous decline in mainline church attendance became noticeable, sociologists documented what was happening. Religious switching continues to be a huge and fertile field in social science research.

For example, one early study in the 1960s revealed marriage was a frequent cause of religious switching. The spouse with the strongest denominational attachment normally determines which church the couple identifies with in the future. A scale was developed that ranks the denominations most likely to lose out in a marriage-choice situation. Roman Catholics are most likely to switch because of marriage, followed by Episcopalians and then Lutherans.[14]

Today the best studies related to adolescent and emerging adult religious shifting comes from the National Study of Youth and Religion and the Jesus Survey. Other sources such as the General Social Survey and the Baylor Religion Survey of 2005 also make positive contributions.

National Study of Youth and Religion. Five years after the National Study of Youth and Religion, which began in 2002 and was completed in 2003, an extensive follow-up study was done with the same youths, now eighteen to twenty-three and termed "emerging adults." While most young people continued to identify with the religion of their parents, emerging adults who identified themselves as Protestants declined 7 percent (from 53% to 46%), and those who identified themselves as Roman Catholic declined 6 percent (from 24% to 18%). Thus Roman Catholics and Protestants had lost the allegiances of 13 percent of those in the study. Interestingly, those who identified themselves as "not religious" increased by exactly 13 percent (from 14% to 27%).[15]

We don't know what *nonreligious* specifically means from the research. It could mean religion is no longer important to them, but it could also mean they retain an amalgamation of religious beliefs but no longer attend any church.

Among the many tables in this 2007–2008 National Study of Youth and Religion we can establish the traditions the newly nonreligious came out of. (We'll consider nones again in chapter seven, including ways they are reachable.)

Table 3.2. Percentage of 13- to 17-year-olds by Religious Tradition Who Left That Tradition and Became Nonreligious as 18- to 23-year-olds

conservative Protestant	15%
mainline Protestant	24%
black Protestant	11%
Roman Catholic	20%
Jewish	37%
Morman	17%
other religions	30%

Source: Christian Smith and Melinda Denton, *Soul Searching* (New York: Oxford University Press, 2005), p. 109.

We see in table 3.2 that conservative, black Protestants and Mormons had losses of under 20 percent, while mainline, Roman Catholic, Jewish and other religions experiences losses of 20 percent or greater.

The 2007–2008 National Study of Youth and Religion also asked emerging adults about their beliefs relating to religious pluralism. Since the same people were interviewed in both studies, we can compare attitudes of religious exclusivity compared to five years prior (see table 3.3).

In question 1 we see three perspectives—"only one religion is true" (traditional), "many religions may be true" (modern) and "there is little truth in any religion" (postmodern)—and the shifting attitudes over five years. Forty-five percent of conservative Protestant eighteen- to twenty-three-year-olds held the traditional perspective, which was down slightly (2%) a half-decade later. Mainline Protestants and Roman Catholics were down 4 percent. Some conservative Protestants might look at the change and be satisfied that it dropped only 2 percent. Others would be aghast at the first number, that slightly less than half (45%) of their eighteen- to twenty-three-year-olds believe only one religion, presumably theirs, is true. In any case, both the traditional and modern views shrank while the postmodern view has grown.

Table 3.3. National Study of Youth and Religion: Beliefs of US Emerging Adults About Religious Exclusivity, Ages 18 to 23

	US	CP	MP	RC	J	LDS	BP
Q1. Beliefs about the truth of one's religion							
Only one religion is true	29%	45%	22%	38%	11%	60%	38%
(percent change)	-2%	-4%	-4%	-4%	4%	-5%	4%
Many religions may be true	57%	45%	66%	49%	53%	32%	66%
(percent change)	-2%	0%	-1%	-1%	-24%	9%	-11%
There is very little truth in religion	12%	7%	12%	13%	36%	8%	8%
(percent change)	4%	4%	7%	5%	21%	1%	4%
Q2. It's OK to pick and choose religious beliefs without having to accept teachings of faith as a whole							
Agree	52%	40%	61%	61%	8%	37%	37%
Percent change in 5 years	7%	8%	8%	8%	-11%	8%	2%

US = all US youth, CP = conservative Protestant, MP = mainline Protestant, RC = Roman Catholic, J = Jewish, LDS = Mormon, BP = black Protestant

Source: Christian Smith and Melinda Denton, *Soul Searching* (New York: Oxford University Press, 2005), p. 135. A recent study of adults tells a similar story, with 83 percent of Roman Catholic adults doubting their religion is the only way. Seventy-nine percent of mainline Protestants were similarly pluralistic in their outlook. See Robert Putnam and David Cambell, *American Grace* (New York: Simon & Schuster, 2010), p. 536.

In question 2 we get at the heart, at least statistically speaking, of the impulse to pick and choose beliefs. Now 40 percent of conservative Protestant youth, and 61 percent of mainline and Roman Catholic youth connect with the à la carte approach to religious faith, and these numbers are up considerably from five years earlier.

The NSYR follow-up also asked the conservative, mainline and Roman Catholic respondents if they engaged in religious practices outside of Christianity. Other practices included aspects of Buddhism, Hinduism, Zen, Wicca, witchcraft or other pagan religions. Five percent of conservative Protestant youth, 15 percent of mainline youth and 9 percent of Roman Catholic youth did.[16]

The NSYR is certainly not the only research effort helping us understand the contours of adolescent belief. Let's examine some others.

Jesus Survey. The Jesus Survey was conceived in the mind of Mike Nappa, who surveyed the teenage workers of the high-profile youth missions organization Reach Workcamps (www.reachwc.org), which involves over eight hundred Christian teenagers in camps that do work, service and outreach projects in ten US states. To participate as a worker or leader in Reach, a teen has to have strong Christian faith and have a willingness to articulate it. Similarly, he or she must be willing to put that faith in action through hard physical work during the summer.[17]

The Jesus Survey included two questions specifically germane to pluralism. Table 3.4 shows the results of the first.

We see then that one-third of these Christian teens held the modern view, that Christianity is not the only way to heaven.

To gain more clarity on the issue, the Jesus Survey asked the question a different way. Question 20 stated, "I am 100% certain that Jesus is the only way to heaven." Fifty-six percent strongly agreed, another 24 percent somewhat agreed and the remaining 20 percent either strongly or moderately disagreed. Cross-correlations

Table 3.4. Jesus Survey Q19

Do Jesus, Muhammad, Buddha and other great religious leaders all have equal standing in leading people to heaven?

Strongly agree	10%
Somewhat agree	23%
Somewhat disagree	19%
Strongly disagree	48%

Source: Christian Smith and Melinda Denton, *Soul Searching* (New York: Oxford University Press, 2005), p. 73.

were done between the two questions, and the Jesus Survey suggests that 13 percent of the youth firmly believed Jesus in not the only way, 39 percent were unsure about the issue, and 49 percent were sure.

The Jesus Survey results from questions 19-20 can be seen as consistent with the NSYR results. This survey also looked at denominational differences. Denominations represented in large enough numbers are delineated in table 3.5. The differences are obvious.

Table 3.5. Jesus Survey: Teen Opinions About Salvation
Is Jesus the only way to salvation? (percent by denomination)

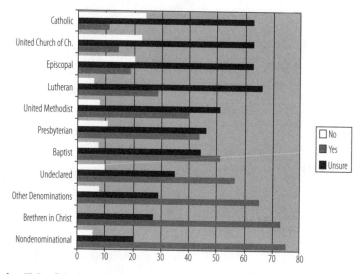

Source: Mike Nappa, *The Jesus Survey* (Grand Rapids: Baker Books, 2012), p. 79.

In looking at the statistics of these tables, we can posit that youth who do not believe Jesus is the only way or who are unsure are open to a syncretistic religious faith.

Other questions queried strength of belief in the trustworthiness of the Bible, the divinity of Jesus and Jesus' resurrection. Table 3.6 shows the numbers of youth who had "strong confidence" in all four basic tenets of the Christian faith.[18]

Baylor Religion Survey. The Baylor Religion Survey provides us with more data regarding the context of adolescent faith and beliefs about other religions. Funded by the Templeton Foundation, the survey included only those ages eighteen and older in a national sample. The results are telling (see table 3.7).

More than half of the respondents held "tolerant" or "modern" views. Little wonder young people believe as they do.

The quantitative data provides a clear picture. Let's now look from another angle.

À la carte faith in cultural trends and sociological theory. The authors of the NSYR do not blame the ebbing of the historic Christian faith on heretical preaching or even anemic teaching in youth groups. Rather, they place the blame squarely on public education.

Table 3.6. Jesus Survey: Confidence in All Four Key Doctrines of the Christian Faith

nondenominational	36%
other denominations	26%
Baptist	17%
Presbyterian	12%
Brethren in Christ	5%
United Methodist	5%
undeclared	3%
Catholic	1%
Episcopal	0%
Lutheran	0%
United Church of Christ	0%

Source: Christian Smith and Melinda Denton, *Soul Searching* (New York: Oxford University Press, 2005), p. 89.

Table 3.7. Baylor Religion Survey Question 25

Which one statement comes closest to your personal view of religious salvation?

My religion is the one true faith that leads to salvation.	19.6%
Many religions lead to salvation.	52.9%
I do not believe in religious salvation.	16.7%
I don't know.	10.7%

Source: The Baylor University Religion Survey 2005, accessed November 25, 2012, www.thearda.com/QuickStats/QS_64.asp.

Nearly all teens seem to have adopted a posture of civility and careful ambiguous inclusiveness when discussing religion. . . . It is also obvious that, in all of this, public schools have served an effective training ground for teaching teenagers to be civil, inclusive, and non-offensive when it comes to faith and spiritual matters.[19]

Nappa observes, "The overarching value of supposed tolerance for other religions has somehow trumped the value of truth, making it natural for our Christian students to actually deny their own beliefs when they may be perceived (whether rightly or wrongly) as intolerant."[20]

A parallel cultural trend is that religion is only one of many social institutions competing for the finite attention of adolescents. School, sports and television have been part of the scene for decades. Today adolescent time and attention is additionally taxed by video games, smartphones, Facebook, Twitter and so on. Smith and Denton observe,

> Religion clearly operates in a social-structurally weak position. . . . If we conceive of adolescents' lives as bundles of finite interest, energy, and investment, then we can think of the various social institutions that touch adolescents' lives as seeking to lay claim to shares of those resources.[21]

The competition-for-youth-attention model sees young people as simply not paying enough attention to religious teaching to notice that significant theological differences exist among competing religions. The default teenage opinion easily becomes "religions are all pretty much about the same thing."

Five years after the first study, the authors of the NSYR were able to look at the data related to emerging adults and articulate a more comprehensive analysis of the predominate mindset of this age group. The data suggests that vocabularies of simple "tolerance" and "cultural competition" are insufficient descriptors. Rather, emerging adults can be described as having a difficult time seeing objective reality beyond themselves. They understand their own experiences, opinions and preferences as the dominant (if not the only) reality. Beyond that, in the words of Smith and Snell,

Most have great difficulty grasping the idea that a reality that is objective to their own awareness or construction of it may exist that could have a significant bearing on their lives. In philosophical terms most emerging adults functionally (meaning how they actually think and act, regardless of the theories they may hold) are soft ontological antirealists, epistemological skeptics and perspectivalists, . . . although few would have any conscious idea of what these terms mean. . . . They are de facto doubtful that an identifiable, objective, shared reality might exist across and around all people that can serve as a reliable reference point for rational deliberation and argument.[22]

Simply put, the NSYR demonstrates that most emerging adults have difficulty believing the notion of truth that applies to everyone. It simply does not make sense to them. This is why many now see all religions as equally important or equally superfluous.

This contemporary expression of postmodernism was first expressed by social theorists such as Talcott Parsons, Jürgen Habermas and Michel Foucault. Among the many lines of social theorizing Habermas's theory of communicative action best provides a conceptual foundation for an educational system emphasizing tolerance and that all truth is provisional. For Habermas the spread of knowledge, economic systems or political systems impinge on a person's consciousness or "life world." It is intolerant, according to Habermas, to foist new knowledge or systems on others, and it makes no sense to do so since one person's "truth" is no more valid than anyone else's truth.

For example, the spread of a capitalist economy into, say, tribal Africa, whose economic systems are tied to tribe, kinship and mutual exchange, has a colonizing effect. Similarly, new ideas or systems imposed from without have a colonizing effect on individuals. "Colonizing my life world" became a pejorative expression for any truth claim (whether a religious truth or an economic or political system) foisted on another with the purpose of changing or influencing that person.[23]

Smith and Snell point out that religion tends to be associated with a "settled life."[24] Social science research has affirmed that major life disruptions may also serve to knock one off their religious (or non-religious) center. This is called the "transition effect." For example, church growth specialists have often recommended churches specifically target newcomers to a community because they may be open to attending church in the first place or to attending church not of the same denomination as their previous location.[25] Most social science literature on the impact of disruption focuses on major life transitions: divorce, death of a family member or job loss. Most adolescents do not experience these in their teenage years, but for those who go to college the disruption list is long: leave home, new living situation, new friends, new ideas, new *everything*. Part of the transition from high school to college may be that the individual meets persons of other faiths. Knowing someone of another religious faith is associated with a more positive attitude about that faith.[26]

Of all sociological theories that intersect religion, rational choice theory has become a well-accepted explanation for how and why people gain, change or lose religious faith. Rational choice, using vocabulary common to economics, posits that the large historic Protestant denominations, as well as Roman Catholicism, have become lazy; that is, they assumed they would always maintain their market share in the United States. When a denomination becomes lazy, it does not bother to understand the changing needs of its "customers." This works as long as the "customers" have no other options, but in a free (religious) market such as the United States, new churches and new denominations have done their homework, so to speak, and know how to meet the customers' felt needs. So, people leave the old and tired denominations and flock to churches that meet their needs.[27] Simply stated, rational choice theory states that people make choices according to their own immediate felt needs. This includes religious choices.

Rational choice theory is germane when it comes to the near disappearance of actual Christianity (as opposed to cultural Christianity) in many Western European nations. State (tax supported) churches do not have to innovate to gain market share and revenue since their coffers are supported by national governments. As a result the church in much of Europe has lost two generations of adherents. Fortunately, there is a resurgence of vital faith among emerging adults in many of these places.[28]

A fine example of a study about adult religious switching was conducted by the Pew Forum on Religion in Public Life, which concluded,

Americans change religious affiliation early and often. In total, about half of American adults have changed religious affiliation at least once during their lives. Most people who change their religion leave their childhood faith before age 24, and many of those who change religion do so more than once. These are among the key findings of a new survey conducted by the Pew Research Center's Forum on Religion & Public Life. The survey documents the fluidity of religious affiliation in the U.S. and describes in detail the patterns and reasons for change. [29]

Rational choice also explains why some youth groups flourish while other youth groups founder. For example, my own PhD dissertation involved the study of five hundred youth groups in four evangelical Protestant denominations. I examined thirty-five variables in three sets: context, leadership and programmatic. My research question was, "What variables, over a two year period of time, correlate significantly with numerical growth in the main youth group weekly gathering?"

I looked at the variables at a certain time and again two years later, particularly looking for the *addition* of leadership or programmatic features correlated with numerical growth. Of the top five variables that correlate with numerical youth group growth, I found one having to do with leadership (the increase in the number of volunteer staff) and two having to do with *program feature* (youth developing a youth-group website, and the addition of sports teams). All three of these can be construed as meeting needs or connecting with natural adolescent interests.[30]

We have looked at a lot of data. Now we will look at biblical and theological perspectives.

À la carte faith and biblical and theological perspectives. The notion of religious pluralism is nothing new from a biblical perspective. Both Old and New Testaments make abundant reference to the religious cultural milieu that is both different from and hostile toward the Abrahamic or nascent Christian faiths. There are also ample cases of persons who attempted to combine the disparate faiths that surrounded them.

Think of Gideon, the hero of Judges 7, believing (perhaps while trembling) that God would provide victory over the Midianites despite his small army of three hundred. The battle went well, and Gideon deflected the popular opinion that he should be a king. Unfortunately, Gideon allowed a great quantity of plundered gold to be gathered. He commission a sacred apron (ephod) to be made (Judg 8:25-27) and allowed (or led?) the worship of this apron. Apparently Gideon was comfortable in believing in both the power of God and the power of his newly manufactured idol. The author of Judges states this golden apron "became a snare to Gideon and his family" (v. 27). Not exactly a ringing endorsement of a God-plus perspective!

We see a New Testament example in the book of Acts when it did not turn out well for some of the Jewish preachers who were jealous of the apostle Paul's preaching and its *power*. Apparently the practice of exorcism was especially dramatic. The awe and applause of people was attractive to some of the Jewish men, and they also tried their hand at exorcisms using the formula they heard the apostle using. Seven sons of the Jewish priest Sceva tried their hand at this and found Jesus-plus something did not work as anticipated.[31]

The classic New Testament text of pluralism is Paul's experience in Athens (Acts 17). Paul was well aware that on Greek soil the gospel was in a crowded religious marketplace. In his famous speech he acknowledged this directly: "I see that in every way you are very religious" (v. 22). He acknowledged their religious sensibility and proclivity, but boldly said that everything had changed because of the gospel. Clearly in Paul's mind, Jesus plus the Greek or Roman pantheon is both abhorrent and impossible.

Fast-forwarding to the present day, the authors of the NSYR propose that the dominant faith of adolescents and emerging adults is no longer the historic Christian faith. It is rather a smattering of quasi-religious fumes, endued with a hefty backstory of tolerance and riding on the notionality of the metanarrative congruence of all faiths.

This becomes the latent theological praxis of adolescents and emerging adults, and is called "Moralistic Therapeutic Deism." This new theology is summarized as follows:

1. A God exists who created the world and watches over it.

2. God wants people to be nice, as taught in the Bible and other religions.

3. The goal in life is to be happy and feel good about oneself.

4. God is handy to help resolve a problem, but otherwise religion is not important.

5. Good people go to heaven.[32]

The NSYR authors are not claiming that people are leaving their denominations to join a new religion called Moralistic Therapeutic Deism. Rather Moralistic Therapeutic Deism

> is simply colonizing many established religious traditions and congregations in the United States, which it is becoming the new spirit living in the old body. Its typical embrace and practice is de facto, functional, practical, and tacit, not formal or acknowledged as a distinctive religion.[33]

In the theological realm the move from the Christian faith toward syncretism, the à la carte approach to religious faith, is ultimately about Christology. What do we believe about the person and work of Jesus Christ?

CHRISTOLOGY QUICK TOUR

A good place to begin to understand the historic Christian faith is to see what the creeds say. The Apostles' Creed devotes 69 of its 109 words to the person and work of Christ.

> I believe in Jesus Christ, his only Son, our Lord,
> who was conceived by the Holy Spirit,
> born of the Virgin Mary,
> suffered under Pontius Pilate,
> was crucified, died, and was buried;
> he descended to the dead.
> On the third day he rose again;
> he ascended into heaven,
> he is seated at the right hand of the Father,
> and he will come to judge the living and the dead.[34]

The second article of the Nicene Creed says,

> We believe in one Lord Jesus Christ, the only-begotten Son of

God, begotten of the Father before all worlds, God of God, Light of Light, Very God of Very God, begotten, not made, being of one substance with the Father by whom all things were made; who for us men, and for our salvation, came down from heaven, and was incarnate by the Holy Spirit of the Virgin Mary, and was made man, and was crucified also for us under Pontius Pilate. He suffered and was buried, and the third day he rose again according to the Scriptures, and ascended into heaven, and sits on the right hand of the Father. And he shall come again with glory to judge both the quick and the dead, whose kingdom shall have no end.[35]

It is interesting that neither creed explicitly states that Jesus is the only way to salvation. I believe it was assumed by the early church fathers that creed hearers would see Christ as the one and only way. I once possessed the entire ante-Nicene and post-Nicene fathers' writings as part of my library. The multivolume set ran well over ten thousand pages. I haven't read every word in that series, but I've read a good deal of it, and these early church fathers certainly believed in Jesus as the only way, and many of them died for their beliefs at the hand of Roman officials.

One thousand years later the English Parliament asked its scholars to come up with a longer, more definitive and explicit statement of the Christian faith. The Westminster Confession of Faith (1646) contains eight paragraphs about Christ. The following is the second paragraph:

The Son of God, the second Person in the Trinity, being very and eternal God, of one substance, and equal with the Father, did, when the fullness of time was come, take upon him man's nature, with all the essential properties and common infir-mities thereof; yet without sin: being conceived by the power of the Holy Ghost, in the womb of the Virgin Mary, of her substance. So that two whole, perfect, and distinct natures, the Godhead and the manhood, were inseparably joined together in one person, without conversion, composition, or confusion. Which person is very God and very man, yet one Christ, the only Mediator between God and man.[36]

What was assumed in the early creeds is made explicit in the Westminster Confession: "one Christ, the *only* Mediator between God and man." Many other descriptions and summaries of Christ's work have come down to us from past generations. The following are three examples.

Jesus as Prophet, Priest and King. Foretold by Moses in Deuteronomy 18:15-18 Jesus is seen in the New Testament as Prophet, the one Old Testament prophecies spoke of (e.g., Lk 24:27), and he was himself the revelation of God (Jn 5:19-23). He is Priest in that he is the one acceptable sacrifice, the penalty paid for our sins, described in Hebrews 9:26 and Hebrews 6:19-20. While refusing earthly kingship, he will be seen as King when every knee will bow (Phil 2:10). There have been many prophets, but only one salvation-giving Priest and singularly reigning King.[37]

Jesus as Savior, Sanctifier, Healer and coming King. The Christological framework articulated by A. B. Simpson, founder of what is now known as the Christian and Missionary Alliance, is that Jesus is Savior, Sanctifier, Healer and coming King. Simpson's heart was to reach people who were not Christians, and the core belief that Jesus is the only way impelled him and thousands of others to take the gospel to all peoples. The Christian and Missionary Alliance website expands on the idea of Jesus as Savior:

Jesus is an exclusive Savior. "Salvation is found in no one else, for there is no other name in heaven given to men by which we must be saved" Acts 4:12. Contrary to what contemporary culture tells us, there are not multiple paths to God. There is only one—Jesus Christ.[38]

Jesus as the Suffering Servant. Foretold in Isaiah 53, Jesus suffered during his life and supremely on the cross. Jesus experienced emotional suffering as a result of his heart for the lost, his disappointment over those who left him, and the weight of the sins of the world. His intellectual suffering came as the result of the obstinate disbelief of the religious leaders of his day. Jesus' spiritual suffering came in the hours prior to the cross when he asked his Father to remove this "cup," not to mention the abandonment by his Father while he suffered physically on the cross.[39]

While it may be possible to discuss Christology without touching the "only way" issue, these understandings of Christ explicitly or implicitly see Christ as the *one* way to God the Father.[40]

SUMMARY

We have discussed the fact that many youths are becoming either religious nones or are dabbling in syncretism. For many, religious belief has been reduced to Moralistic Therapeutic Deism, and in the process most of the markers of vital faith are removed or are decidedly lacking.

One of the best expressions of what society has lost as people become less religious, quasi-religious or completely nonreligious comes from atheist Alaine de Botton. With acute understanding he speaks of how Christianity fosters community, kindness, education, tenderness, purpose and a host of other benefits. He remarks,

Secular society has not been able to solve with any particular skill: first, the need to live together in communities in harmony, despite our deeply rooted selfish and violent impulses. And second, the need to cope with terrifying degrees of pain which arise from our vulnerability to professional failure, to troubled relationships, to the death of loved ones and to our own decay and demise. God may be dead, but the urgent issues which impelled us to make him up still stir and demand resolutions.[41]

Is there anything youth workers can do to help prevent young people and emerging adults from watering down their faith to the point of irrelevance? The biblical world was also a multifaith world, and many persons of biblical fame navigated this world successfully, others infamously did not. In chapter four we will look at some biblical examples.

4

CHRISTIANS IN OCCUPIED TERRITORY

The Church Has
Been There, Done That

In Mahwah, New Jersey, there is a busy intersection that is typical of intersections in North America. Yes, there is a Dunkin' Donuts shop and a gas station, but at or near that corner there is also a small Lutheran church, a large charismatic church and a megamosque.

In the Vancouver suburb of Richmond it is not just an intersection but a mile-long stretch of No. 5 Road. The locals call it "Highway to Heaven." The Ling Yen Mountain Buddhist Temple is across the street from the Richmond Bethel Mennonite Church. Nearby is Nanaskar Gudwara Gursikh Temple, and down the road is the Az-Zarhraa Islamic Center. A little farther along one comes to the Richmond Jewish Day School, the Hindu Ram Krishna Center, the Vedic Cultural Centre and the first Tibetan temple in North America, which is also the home base of the Thrangu Monastery. Richmond Christian School is there as well.

I recall as a child asking my parents about other religions as we drove to church. However, by "religions" I (unknowingly) meant *denominations*. On our four-mile drive to Portland Avenue Baptist Church we passed a Lutheran, a Methodist, a Catholic and a Bible church. My question was simple: "Would people *other than Baptists* go to heaven?" My mother indicated that answer was probably no. (She relaxed on that point some years later, however.) Eventually, of course, I became aware of other religions, not only by means of hearing missionary stories at church but by interacting with Hare Krishna members while attending the University of Washington, and interacting with Sikhs, Hindus, Muslims and Jews in the years since.

Christians now live in a world where other religions are both visible and viable in the United States. This basic reality, however, is nothing new. The Hebrew and Christian faiths were born into very robust religious marketplaces. As we help young people and their parents navigate their daily lives, it helps to know that the challenge we face is illustrated, exemplified and amplified in the Old and New Testaments. As we will see, there is considerable connection between the biblical world and today's world in this regard, but there is a huge disconnect as well.

THE OLD TESTAMENT WORLD

The story of God's people begins with the life of Abraham in Genesis 12. Here we see Abraham and family on the move, first to Canaan and then, because of famine, on to Egypt. We know from archaeology and extrabiblical sources that these changes of address put this man and his family in a cultural milieu brimming with gods other than the one true God. The Canaanites were polytheists. They believed in a god for nearly every aspect of their lives: twenty-three gods in all.[1] Three of these, Baal, Dagon and Molek, receive considerable coverage in Scripture. As we can well imagine, it was no small task for Abraham's family to continue believing in one God when everyone around them believed otherwise.

Similarly, Abraham's move to Egypt (Gen 12:10) put his family in a context that was even more polytheistic. Egypt had nearly two thousand gods, some regional, some national, some representing earth creatures, others representing stellar objects. Chief among the Egyptian gods was Amon-Ra, god of the sun.[2] Despite living in this religious stew, Abraham both evidenced and articulated a belief in a single God who actually showed up in his life.

Among many other examples of his positive response to God, Abraham accepted a covenantal relationship with God (Gen 17:9). As a sign of the covenant he required all male members of his household to be circumcised (Gen 17:23) and, unlike Sarah, who took the notion of bearing a child late in life as hilariously improbable, Abraham believed God's promise of a son. And Sarah indeed became pregnant (Gen 21:2).

We can imagine that none of these acts of faith were necessarily easy. We do not know the inner workings of Abraham's mind as he counterculturally believed in one God. Quite probably, however, the story of his willingness to obey God in the sacrifice of his son Isaac brings us close to a spiritually fatal worldview collision for Abraham. In the NIV Study Bible, Genesis 22 is titled "Abraham Tested." What an understatement! When God asked Abraham to slay his young son on the altar, we can imagine his confusion and mixed emotions. Abraham loved his son deeply, and what about God's promise that Abraham would have numerous decedents (Gen 15:5)?

Here it seems God was asking Abraham to worship in the same manner as a worshiper of Molek, that is, by child sacrifice. Abraham's whole adult life had been lived in contrast to the religious culture of his day, and now *this*. However, in testing Abraham's faith, God, who called a last-second halt to the sacrifice, is confirming a faith that is distinctly different. Abraham is called to a distinct faith, belief in the one God who actually shows up and makes a difference time and again.

After Joshua led Israel into Canaan, much of the remaining Old Testament narrative contains a subtext with this as a dominant question: How do we live in this place when everyone around us believes differently than we do?

Did these ancient Hebrews really know and understand the religious beliefs of those around them? They certainly did. The vocabulary of the Old Testament is telling.

Molek, the god who requires child sacrifice, is named nine times.[3] The god Baal is mentioned over one hundred times, and sometimes the locations of Baal altars are noted (Baal Zephon [Ex 14:2] and Bamoth Baal [Num 22:41]). Apparently parents enthusiastically (or at least superstitiously) named their children Baal, such as Baal-Hanon in Genesis 36:38 or Baal Meon in Numbers 32:38.[4]

The Canaanite god Dagon is connected to crop fertility and is mentioned eight times. Dagon is the darling god of the Philistines, Israel's nemesis in the Old Testament books of Judges and 1 Samuel. Old Testament literature is rather sparse when it comes to actual humor, but Dagon temples in Philistia become a source of great hilarity as told in 1 Samuel 4–6. The basic story, which illustrates well Hebrew knowledge of other religions, is as follows.

The Israelites were, it seems, in a constant state of war or near war with their neighbors the Philistines. One of the Hebrew elders suggested that in the face of the most recent defeat by the Philistines, they ought to bring out their secret weapon: the Ark of the Covenant.[5] Much to the disappointment of the Israelite army, the Ark didn't work as a weapon and was captured by the Philistines. The Ark, then, became a disconcertingly real "issue" for the Philistines.

Philistine decision makers first put the Ark in the temple of Dagon in the town of Ashdod. Big problem! The next morning the statue of Dagon had fallen down (bad enough) and the people in the town were stricken with tumors (some scholars think the proper translation is *hemorrhoids*), and there were rats everywhere. The Ark was moved from town to town, and in every case the result was the same:

broken Dagon, hemorrhoids and rats. Finally, the Philistines sent it back on a cart to the Israelites, having put as a peace offering a few golden rats and hemorrhoids in the Ark with the tablets. This story, told and retold, must have seemed hilarious to those listening. Those poor Philistines, *ha ha.*

The writer of 1 Samuel divulges a few details which demonstrates the detailed knowledge of this Dagon religion. Apparently when Dagon fell before the Ark at Ashdod, it broke apart over the threshold of the temple. The author points out then, "That is why to this day neither the priests of Dagon nor any others who enter Dagon's temple at Ashdod step on the threshold" (1 Sam 5:5). Many hundreds of years later the Israelites are still aware of Dagon temple details, as the Prophet Zephaniah mentions those who "avoid stepping on the threshold" as a widespread practice in the land, and that Jews should not do it (Zeph 1:9).

Many other gods appear in the pages of the Old Testament. Asherah, the mother god, is mentioned forty times; high places for other god worship, over seventy times; and general idols are mentioned and warned against over 140 times.

The point is, the Old Testament people of God were trying to be faithful to Yahweh and in an environment chockfull of other religious choices—just like Christian young people and their families today.

A very poignant Old Testament statement of faith is profoundly given in Psalm 121:1-3. David says,

I lift up my eyes to the mountains,
    where does my help come from?

Not stated but very possibly in his mind was the thought, *No, it's not that Asherah pole over there, or that Molek altar on that hill, or that temple of Dagan you can see, but rather*

My help comes from the LORD,
    the Maker of heaven and earth.
He will not let your foot slip.

THE NEW TESTAMENT WORLD

Like their Hebrew counterparts, early Christians came to faith while living in a very multicultural and multireligious setting.

We know from the book of Acts and the Epistles that the early church was urban. This social fact helps scholars such as Wayne Meeks, David Horrell and Larry Hurtado explain and account for the growth and normative practices of the early church.[6]

Many aspects of this New Testament world seem familiar to us in the twenty-first century. The Roman world had a common currency, hot tubs, fast food, shopping malls, extensive (and safe) travel, labor unions, international trade, high taxes, mail, professional sports and individually ticketed seats in coliseums seating forty thousand, career tracks, government bureaucracy, apartment living, running water, heated floors, political intrigue, vacation homes and villas with a view.[7]

Early Christianity and the Roman religious world often intersected. Paul comments on the religious statues around Athens in his famous words "People of Athens! I see that in every way you are very religious" (Acts 17:22). We see also in Acts that the increasing number of Christians was hurting retail sales in a whole sector of the economy in Ephesus—the manufacture of travel souvenirs depicting the Greek goddess Artemis. Regarding this, Demetrius, a pagan silversmith and entrepreneur, gathered other craftsmen and shopkeepers and said, "You see and hear how this fellow Paul has convinced and led astray a large number of people here in Ephesus and in practically the whole province of Asia. He says that gods made by human hands are *no gods at all*" (Acts 19:23-27).[8]

Just as in the Old Testament, there are many warnings against falling prey to the allures and temptations of the Greco-Roman culture. The New Testament writers seem to have had the same question as the Old Testament writers: How do we live in this place when everyone around us believes differently than we do?

It's hard to imagine what it would have been like to be a Christian in the Roman world.

Christians certainly faced *misunderstanding*. The words of Jesus "whoever eats my flesh and drinks my blood" (Jn 6:56) were understood by Christians to have symbolic meaning in the bread and wine of Communion. To non-Christians though, these words were shocking and repugnant. Additionally, especially in the early years people thought it very strange that Christians believed in only one God. Christians were an anomaly in a world where most people wanted to cover all their bases in life by believing in many gods. In this respect Christ followers were seen as curiously less religious than most people.[9]

Christians faced *sexual temptation* in a culture awash with not only pornography and legal prostitution, but pagan-temple fundraising involving sex for financial donation and worship via sex. Brothels dotted the urban landscape of most cities in the Roman world. Since they were legal establishments (and taxed by city government), they spared no expense to advertise with lurid drawings, sayings and, if street frontage was large enough, display of available girls. Funding of pagan temples was enhanced through temple prostitution. The annual festival of Venus held in April was of particular note. One pagan religion, the cult of Aphrodite, required all its female adherents to have sexual intercourse with a stranger at least once in their life, preferably on the front steps of the temple while others looked on.[10]

Little wonder that Paul repeatedly warns Christians to remain sexually pure. In one letter his warning includes a reference to pagan practices: "You should avoid sexual immorality; . . . each of you should learn to control your own body in a way that is holy and honorable, not in passionate lust like the pagans, who do not know God" (1 Thess 4:3-5).

Misunderstanding, mockery and sexual temptation. Early Christians felt very much like a minority in their cultural context. Sound familiar? How do we help youth and families navigate these waters? We will consider this in chapters five, seven and eight.

Christians knew they were different. Most Christians would not swear allegiance to Caesar (their first and highest loyalty was to Christ). They would not acknowledge Caesar as divine. This was no big deal to emperors like Trajan and Hadrian (A.D. 98–138), brilliant military leaders and strategic thinkers, who were too busy to care about such silliness. On the other hand, emperors with fragile egos or who lacked assurance desired acknowledgment of their divinity. Christians, an identifiable subpopulation in the Roman world, were officially persecuted, often brutally. The emperor Nero blamed the ills of the city on Christians and infamously hoisted many Christians on poles, burned them alive and enjoyed the street lighting this provided.

The rise of Christianity in the Roman world from the birth of the church in A.D. 33 to the purported conversion of Emperor Constantine in the early 300s is a subject of interest to historians and sociologists. How and why did the Christian church grow from 120 persons (Acts 1:15) to an estimated 30 million in three hundred years? Why not the worship of Mithras, Sibyl or any number of the religions that were thriving as the church was born? This is not simply an academic question. The answer may inform our own youth ministry in today's pluralistic culture.

Sociologist Rodney Stark suggests the primary reason is that Christians were simply different. They lived in a manner different from their not-yet-Christian neighbors and work associates, and many of those differences were obvious much of the time.[11]

Different in what respects?

First, says Stark, Christians did not practice infanticide or abortion, and thus had a higher birthrate over time than others. Urban dwellers who could afford it had access to abortion, and the practice was not uncommon. Though abortion is not explicitly mentioned in any apostolic letter or Gospel teaching, Christians connected the dots and avoided these practices. Infanticide, that is, tossing newborns (usually females) onto the garbage heaps or, alternatively, just exposing them to the elements without care, was one way urban people tried to cope with overcrowding in their apartments.

Second, when Christians were tortured or killed for entertainment, it was a profoundly disturbing experience for many onlookers. Christians seemed *happy* facing death. Christians, as a group, when facing the lions or burning, often *sang*. Onlookers went back to their apartments in confused wonder, *Why did my neighbor sing when the fire was lit? I really liked my Christian neighbors, why are they being killed? What do Christ followers have that I don't?*[12]

Third, and most salient from Stark's point of view, is what Christians did when plagues swept the Roman world beginning in the late second century. When individuals began to show symptoms of plague, it was not uncommon for people in the neighborhood, including family members, to flee the city. Some cities became virtually depopulated within a week. Plague victims were left to die alone.

Some Christians also died, of course, but the striking truth is most Christians stayed behind in the cities *to care for their plague-stricken friends, neighbors and total strangers.* Stark points out that given proper nursing care (food, shelter, water) about 20 percent of afflicted people recovered from plague.

Suppose you had the plague. Suppose your family fled in panic when you got the spots on your skin. Suppose one of your last memories before you sank into feverish incoherence was some Christian neighbors gently carrying you into their home. Suppose you woke up one bright day, fever gone, to a room full of smiling faces. Would your first words be "I'd like to give thanks to Mithras"? Apparently most recovered plague victims woke and, for all practical purposes, said, "What must I do to be saved?"

Christians thus had a reputation of being good and caring people who could be trusted. They had a higher purpose in life, lived to please Christ in this world and looked forward to being with him in the next.

As the numbers of Christians increased, the numbers of followers of the Greek, Egyptian or Roman pantheon shrank. In the second half of the fourth century, after Christianity became the de facto religion of the Roman world, the emperor Julian tried to resurrect paganism. He wrote exasperated letters to the leaders of the few pagan temples that still existed in the empire, pleading, "Can't you teach people who still believe in our gods to be nice [like Christians]?" In another letter he exclaims to his pagan priests, "These impious Galileans not only feed their own poor, but ours also; welcoming them into their agape, they attract them, as children are attracted, with cakes."[13]

TODAY: LINKAGE AND DISJUNCTURE

We have seen how the Hebrews in the Old Testament and Christians in the New Testament era lived their faith in a context rife with other religious choices. The same is true today. However, our day and the day of the Hebrews and early Christians are vastly different. Ancient Jews and Christians knew they were different from their pagan neighbors, and they had considerable knowledge of the religious beliefs and practices of the others around them. They felt no shame in being different. The early Christians most likely came to faith as adults and were baptized in a very public setting. They had a very distinct before-and-after conversion testimony.

It appears that most Christian young people today do not understand their own faith, let alone the faith (or nonfaith) of others. And many young people (and their parents) loathe being different from peers. In the mighty quest to "fit in" they jettison any aspect of the Christian faith that causes them to stand out.

HOUSTON, WE HAVE A PROBLEM

There was a big explosion and gages went berserk. Unbeknown at first to the astronauts aboard Apollo 13, their spacecraft was venting oxygen—not only oxygen to power their fuel cells but also for them to breath. The movie *Apollo 13* depicts the frantic attempts to figure out what just went wrong and what to do about it.

Christian Smith and Melinda Denton's *Soul Searching* has been a "Houston, we have a problem" moment for the church and for youth ministry. The National Study of Youth and Religion, described in *Soul Searching*, revealed that most adolescents who would identify themselves as Christian have only the slimmest grasp of what the Christian faith actually entails.

Our culture has produced young people who "typically consider themselves to be self-directing, autonomous individuals, the key mediators or arbiters of all outside influences, fully in charge of their own interests, choices, and actions."[14] Outcomes of this pervasive attitude affect adolescent faith (or lack thereof) in three important respects. According to Smith and Denton, most adolescents (1) view religion as not relevant to their lives now, (2) are very hesitant to expose personal religious beliefs in public, and (3) the adolescent world is full of so many more visible and more important things (such as sports, music, drama club, a part-time job, and a bevy of TV shows or movies that must be viewed) that there is little motivation (or energy) to consider deep issues of faith or spirituality.[15]

Smith and Denton are hesitant to even call the faith of American adolescence Christian. Rather, as we saw earlier, they use the term Moralistic Therapeutic Deism. Smith and Denton had data regarding the denominational background of the more than two thousand youth interviewed. Youth from liberal Protestant and Roman Catholic homes generally had an abysmal grasp of the Christian faith. On the other hand, young people of conservative denominations possessed vocabulary to articulate the what, why and how of the Christian faith. Subsequent research and follow-up publications stemming from the National Study of Youth and Religion have affirmed and given greater nuance to the original findings.[16] In chapters seven and eight we will consider many proactive moves youth leaders can take to make it more likely our youth will understand the Christian faith and their own role in re-presenting Christ to their peers.

SUMMARY

In this chapter I have provided a historical perspective of being a believer in a context where most people are not. Our situation is not that much different from that of the Old and New Testaments. We too are surrounded by people of other faiths or no faith at all. Hand-wringing is uncalled for. The church has been there, done that, for centuries.

Unlike the biblical and early church eras, however, today many Christians, young and old, have a perilously shallow understanding of faith. Before presenting proactive solutions to this problem, we first need to clarify our understanding of *pluralism* and *multifaith society* (chap. 5), which makes a difference in how we conceptualize and carry out youth ministry. Clearly this is an important issue not only for the church but the personal flourishing of the young people in our own student ministries (chap. 6).

5

THEOLOGY IN PRAXIS:
LATENT OR ARTICULATED VIEWS
OF MULTIFAITH SOCIETY

Youth Ministry on Purpose

Students with no Christian background routinely attended our youth group meetings. Their parents were Jewish, new age or nones. Cortney began coming to our junior high group at the invitation of a friend, and she seemed to enjoy it. She came back regularly for several months, and I got to know her better through hangout time and playing amoeba tag, capture the flag, sit down backwards basketball, volleyball and so forth. It quickly became apparent that Cortney was not from a Christian background and had no knowledge of the Bible or its stories. She used rough language and seemed to know the lyrics of every secular song about sex, and enjoyed rattling off the lurid lyrics to shock our homeschooled kids. Poured into her clothes, Cortney was a typical "twelve going on twenty." In our "together time," where the Bible is presented, Cortney began to show some engagement with what was going on, in an aloof, oh-so-hip kind of way.

I was leading the Bible study portion of our weekly meeting and out of the blue she asked, "Will I go to hell if I have sex before marriage?" This was *way off* the topic of the night, and I told her I'd answer her later. During snack time she asked me again. Years earlier I would have used the opportunity to present the biblical view of sex and lead right in to something along the lines of "Cortney, God loves you and has a wonderful plan for your life." That would have been a very *traditional* approach. A more *modern* approach would be to unpack different approaches to the salvation question with the goal of helping her understand her choices in the matter. Instead, I came at the situation in a more *postmodern* way. I said, "Good question, bring it up again in a week or two." She looked a little befuddled and walked off.

Next week, she sought me out as soon as I arrived. "Will I go to hell if I have sex before marriage?" My answer? "Well, Cortney, whether or not you go to heaven or hell kinda depends on *who you know*, not *what you do*." And with that I walked off to play Ping-Pong with some of the boys. Her wide eyes displayed her confusion.

The following week I approached her. "So, Cortney, have you figured it out yet?" "No." She frowned. Then I gave her a few sentences about knowing Jesus and again walked away, leaving her standing there.

Two weeks passed and the group was playing frozen tag on the basketball court. I happened to be "frozen" about five feet from where she was similarly frozen.

"Say, Cortney, do you know him yet?"

"I'm afraid."

"Good! I think you're getting close."

Almost immediately I was "unfrozen" and ran off.

Later that evening someone else on the staff was leading the Bible study. Cortney raised her hand in the middle and asked, "How do you know Jesus?"

This was way off topic, but Mark, who was leading that night, responded, "Good question." He turned toward the group (these are kids ages 11-13) and asked, "Would any of you like to answer Cortney's question?" About six kids raised their hands and one by one contributed their thoughts about what it means to come to have a relationship with Christ.

Mark thanked them for their responses and returned to the topic of the evening.

What happened afterward is amazing. Brent, whose physical appearance was the opposite of Cortney's, was twelve but looked nine. Brent often has a blank look on his face that seems to say, "Notice, the lights are on but no one is home." Well, that night, the lights were on and someone was home.

After the meeting ended, Brent took Cortney into a side room, explained the plan of salvation, and prayed with her to receive Christ! She came out with tears of joy. And over the weeks we all saw a complete transformation in her. She was no longer cold, hard, edgy and proudly sexual. We watched the fruit of the Spirit begin to form in her life. *Everyone* could see the difference in her life.

This chapter explores three primary perspectives on religious ministry in a multifaith society. The traditional, modern and postmodern perspectives make a difference when it comes to youth work. A multifaith perspective can be latent; that is, someone might not be aware she or he is working out of a certain theological worldview. Others, though, might be very aware of their theological stance related to religious pluralism. Each perspective has implications for youth work praxis.

THEOLOGICAL UNDERSTANDING AFFECTS YOUTH MINISTRY PRAXIS

Social scientists measure the effects of theologies on ministry practice by comparing denominations. Though convenient, this is also problematic.

I will use the theological labels "liberal," "mainline," "evangelical" and "conservative" for convenience.[1] An evangelical or conservative denomination would interpret Scripture from a traditional Christian framework, believing that salvation is mediated only through Christ. A church from a more liberal denomination may be less likely to teach Christ as the only way because it appears intolerant of other faith communities.

On the other hand the liberal-conservative distinction is problematic in that not all churches in a "liberal" denomination are theologically liberal. There are many Methodist, Presbyterian, Lutheran and Episcopal churches that proclaim Christ as the one and only way to salvation.[2]

The architects of the National Study of Youth and Religion have chosen, however, to use the denominations as representative types, and they expanded the list to include Roman Catholic and black Protestants. The specific denominations are named in the study's footnotes.[3]

The NSYR is a good place to consider denominational difference and youth ministry emphases and outcomes. The NSYR found a spectacular variance among young people raised in these denominations when it comes to understanding and articulating a Christian faith. That variance actually follows very closely what Dean Kelly found in 1972: youth of liberal/mainline denominations were barley able to identify themselves as "Christian" let alone articulate it or see faith as having any relevance to their lives. On the other hand, the more evangelical/conservative denominational youth were able to identify the basic tenets of the Christian faith, and many were able to articulate a living faith that made a difference in daily life.[4]

The NSYR included in their surveys and interviews questions related to religious pluralism. Significant differences are immediately apparent as denominational types are set side by side (see table 5.1).

Table 5.1. Religious Particularism and Individualism Among US Adolescents, Ages 13 to 17

	US	CP	MP	BP	RC
Beliefs about religion's truth					
Only one religion is true	29%	46%	26%	31%	19%
Many religions may be true	60%	48%	67%	63%	71%
There is very little truth in religion	9%	4%	5%	4%	9%
Beliefs about religious particularity					
People should practice only one faith	46%	59%	38%	57%	40%
OK to practice religions besides one's own	51%	36%	59%	40%	58%
Beliefs about conversion attempts					
OK for religious people to try to convert others	54%	70%	58%	54%	43%
Everyone should leave others alone	43%	27%	39%	42%	55%
OK to pick and choose aspects of different faiths for oneself without accepting the whole	46%	36%	53%	34%	54%

(US = all US youth, CP = conservative Protestants, MP = mainline Protestants, BP = black Protestants, RC = Roman Catholic)

Source: Adapted from Christian Smith and Melinda Lundquest Denton, *Soul Searching* (New York: Oxford University Press, 2005), p. 74.

Some conservative Protestants may be upset that only 46 percent of their youth think a single religion—Christianity—is true. Compared to mainline and Roman Catholic youth, however, conservative Protestant young people generally lean to the traditional/historic religious stance, while a much higher percentage of the youth in mainline and Roman Catholic churches reflect a modern stance. It is interesting to note that a measurable percent of young people seemingly embrace the postmodern stance, given their positive response to "There is very little truth in religion."

Undoubtedly the denominational reactions to these results were varied. Conservatives and evangelicals would find the numbers shocking and alarming. Some mainline Protestants may have been satisfied that their young people reflect an enlightened and modern perspective. The day the NSYR data was published probably was not a good day for Roman Catholic bishops. By definition Roman Catholics are traditional, and yet they seem to be producing the fewest percentage of young people who maintain the historic Christian faith.[5]

Other studies have produced similar findings in the United States as well as in other countries. A study of 269 church-based youth groups in Indiana, for example, revealed that the purpose and programming varied widely across denominational categories.[6] For example, while 95 percent of the youth groups in the survey had retreats and service projects, only 53 percent had mission trips, only 34 percent had some kind of adult leadership structure to give oversight and encouragement to youth workers, and only 63 percent had any youth activities or events scheduled for the month in which the survey was conducted. And a study of 275 Roman Catholic parishes around Detroit found that adults in these parishes felt an urgent need for a greater emphasis on youth ministry leadership and programming. Perhaps these people already sensed, from their own children, the diminution of faith.[7]

A major study among rural churches in eight denominations from the Northern Plains states examined evangelical Protestant, mainline Protestant and Catholic denominations. Among these churches, evangelical Protestants were much more likely to have active youth programs with higher participation rates. Catholic youth groups were more likely to be led by paid youth workers and participate in ecumenical activities. Mainline youth ministries were much more likely to be led by the senior pastor because of the lack volunteers or financial resources to hire a youth pastor.[8]

Another US-based study leaned primarily on the National Longitudinal Survey of Adolescent Health (known as the ADD). The ADD's statistical sampling approach assured highly reliable representative results, and their survey included many questions about faith and religious affiliation. The author of this research was able to cross-compare participation rates with church and denominational growth (or decline) rates. The results? The greater percentage of a denomination's young people who were actively engaged in a church youth group, the greater the numerical growth of that denomination over the ten-year period of 1995–2005. Evangelical Protestants (including charismatics) saw denominational growth, and mainline denominations saw decline during the same period.[9]

A study based in Melbourne, Australia, held in-depth interviews with five Roman Catholic youth workers, three Anglican youth workers and four Uniting (evangelical) youth workers. The authors were struck by the very real differences in how these three categories of youth workers viewed the purpose, role and program of church youth work. For example, the Roman Catholic ministries focused heavily on helping youth know and experience the meaning of the sacraments and understanding God's mercy and what it means in terms of obligation to work for social justice. The Protestant youth workers seemed less concerned about theological foundations and more concerned about "doing something." On the other hand, Protestant youth ministries heavily focused on youth "ownership" of the youth program and feeling empowered. This aspect of youth ministry was not articulated by the Roman Catholic youth workers. Again, theological context seems to make a difference in youth ministry praxis.[10]

We have looked at youth ministry practice outcomes based on denominational differences. The following is an empirical study that used direct measurements of theological perspective not mediated by denominational affiliation.

In 2006 I was engaged in a research project to discover the differences and commonalities among church-based youth ministries in every continent. One of my interests was to explore theology and youth ministry practice. What better way than to consider the subject of infant baptism, the "waters that divide" the church?[11]

Table 5.2. Youth Ministries Within Churches That Practice Infant Baptism Compared to Those That Do Not

	Baptize infants	Do not baptize infants
Size of group: percent indicating 150-500	38%	62%
Have outreach events 1-4 times per month	47%	69%
Youth leading more than half of each meeting	36%	45%
Have a mission/vision/core values statement	64%	87%

(N = 298, 171 baptize infants, 127 do not)

Source: Len Kageler, "A Cross National Analysis of Church Based Youth Ministries," *Journal of Youth Ministries* 8, no. 2 (spring 2010): 49-68.

We see here a clear theology-praxis link. Churches who do not baptism infants but see their children and youth as lost and needing to be saved have much larger youth groups, have more outreach events, have young people themselves leading meetings more often, and are more likely to have a mission/purpose statement.[12]

Let's examine youth ministries that are clearly represent one perspective or the other.

THE TRADITIONAL VIEW

What does Cortney's story have to do with pluralism and multifaith student ministry?

The youth pastor and volunteers in our youth ministry hold a traditional, historic Christian view of religious pluralism, which is often referred to as exclusivism. That is, while there may be beauty, goodness and value in other religions, they are not the way to God. The only way to know God is through Jesus Christ and his sacrifice on the cross.[13] Given this foundation, our entire youth ministry is about loving young people into a personal relationship with Christ, walking with them as they learn to live it out in community, and helping them learn to share their faith with others.

How else do we see the traditional view evidenced in our youth ministry?

First, the youth pastor and the five volunteers (including me) firmly believe that *God uses youth*. We believe twelve-year-olds are capable of knowing Jesus, and once they have committed their lives to him they have the Holy Spirit in their lives and are able to experience God's direction. They are able to re-present Jesus in their own lives, as did twelve-year-old Brent in his conversion conversation with Cortney.

Of course, not all youth in traditional-leaning youth ministries do this well. I could fill a chapter with horror stories of good kids acting out. For example, a few months after Cortney's conversion I came in from the basketball court and found Troy simulating having sex with the couch—not *on* the couch but sex *with* the couch. (This situation is not covered in any youth ministry books I've read!)

I firmly told him to stop and informed him this was not appropriate youth group behavior and that if he persisted he would need to go home. He desisted and was a pretty normal (and nice) thirteen-year-old boy the rest of the night.

Despite their missteps, failure and shocking setbacks, however, we see Jesus in most of them much of the time, and we believe we are all equal in this sense: the ground is level at the foot of the cross. Whether we are thirteen or a *much* older college professor, we are all trying to figure out how to live the Christian life on a daily basis. Furthermore, we all mess up some of the time. Most of these kids know their leaders are walking with them, not above or behind them. In this youth group, they sense they are valued.

Second, the traditional view is implied in five key features of our youth ministry.

We *meet* as youth come to the weekly gathering, having heard from their friends that it is interesting, a lot of fun, and they'll feel accepted. Newcomers are welcome at other "meet" events as well, such as a trip to the paintball place.

We *lead* when all are gathered, one of the leaders calls the youth together and some aspect of the Bible is presented creatively and with much student involvement. This takes place in Sunday school as well, where the explicit focus is spiritual growth.

We *empower* students as they are given leadership opportunities within the student ministry. These opportunities include helping in the worship band, speaking as part of the Bible time or being on the student leadership team, which plans most of the nonweekly events of the group. Students are also empowered as they are taught what it means to share Christ with their peers.

We *release* youth to make disciples in various service-oriented projects, either for a day or, in the summer, for a week, doing simple construction projects in rural West Virginia or leading an evangelistic daily Vacation Bible School for another church.

Among the many advantages of these five ministry aspects is that the youth pastor and volunteer staff are clear about the ministry's purpose. We know the purpose of each aspect of the ministry and how it fits into a larger whole. The metanarrative is leading youth to Christ and discipling them to disciple others. The individual pieces support this overall narrative.[14]

There is no ambiguity about Christ here. Jesus is the one and only way to God. This theological understanding is the foundation for the whole purpose of this youth ministry, and the point specifically comes up in the teaching done within the context of the youth group or Sunday school.

This traditional view, the historic view of the Christian church, is that the Bible pretty much means what it says. However, it is important to distinguish genres of literature. This approach acknowledges that biblical literature includes history, prophecy, poetry and epistles. For example, poetry (e.g., Psalms) uses metaphors whereas history (e.g., Exodus) typically doesn't. In poetry we do not take everything literally. When the psalmist writes in Psalm 63:7 "Because you are my help, I sing under the shadow of your wings," it does not mean that God literally has wings. Furthermore we often need other Scripture to help refine the meaning of a particular text. A good place to begin in biblical understanding is to ask how the original hearers/ readers were likely to understand it.

Using these principles then, many youth workers understand that Jesus taught that he was the only way to God.

- "I am the gate for the sheep. . . . Whoever enters through me will be saved" (Jn 10:7-9).

- "I am the way and the truth, and the life. No one comes unto the Father except through me" (Jn 14:6).

The unique character of Jesus was the reason the apostles and the early church told others about Christ as the only way to salvation. "Salvation is found in no one else, for there is no other name under heaven given to mankind by which we must be saved" (Acts 4:12). This *missional* imperative, then, did not expire at the close of the first century but is the mission of the church and the mission of Christian youth work today.

The youth ministry that led Cortney to Christ does not see missions or evangelism as simply "spiritual scalp hunting" or "saving souls." It emphasizes caring about and serving people because God loves all people, and believers are to re-present Jesus in that selfless service, even if there are no evangelistic results.

Protestant and Roman Catholic scholars are exerting much effort to understand their faith in the context of the "religious other." For example, in 1962 Pope John XII opened the gathering of Catholic Church leaders known as Vatican II. In this great counsel those present reflected on the place of the Christian church in the modern world. Vatican II affirmed that while the Spirit of God is working everywhere in the world, including other religions, these other religions, no matter how noble, do not offer a way to salvation.[15] The Belgian Jesuit priest Jacques Dupuis, after a lifetime of serving the church in non-Western settings, set forth his take on this in the towering work *Toward a Christian Theology of Religious Pluralism*.[16] He expresses his deep appreciation for the depth and beauty found in many other religions.

While all reviewers applaud the book, some are saddened that he does not take the next step, to say that other faith communities also mediate salvation for their adherents. Dupuis does quite the opposite. He rejects the "deabsolutizing" and the "deobjectifying" of the historic church's view of Christ as being the one and way to salvation. He points out that those who make truth relative, situational or only personal are "claiming to enjoy higher ground, above and beyond all the particular perspectives. This, in fact, looks very much like making an absolute objective judgment about the allegedly subjective and relative nature of any truth available to others with their limited world views."[17] He goes on,

> The Christian claim for Jesus Christ, as traditionally understood still stands: faith in Jesus Christ does not merely consist in trusting that he is 'for me' the path to salvation; it means to believe that the world and humankind find salvation in and through him. Nothing short of this does justice to the New Testament massive assertions.[18]

Let's look at a second perspective on religious pluralism.

THE MODERN VIEW

Many churches and their Christian youth ministries happily affirm their Christian faith but also affirm there are other equally valid ways to know God. For example, a large Congregational church in Illinois says, "We are grounded in tradition, centered in worship, called to serve and free to dream. We believe that everyone is a child of God."[19] Their ministry includes a large pastoral and associate staff, which places a high priority on children's and youth ministries. Their youth pastor, Rachel, has experienced a God-calling into youth work, and she feels at home in ministry at this church for a variety of reasons, especially that its "theology is progressive and reflects that God is still calling us to love kindness, do justice and walk humbly before our God."[20] The vision of their Junior High Fellowship is representative of the other ministries as well. This vision includes "experiencing spiritual practices from a variety of faith traditions during our Spiritual Practice nights."[21]

The Senior High Youth Fellowship is described in part as "a faithful gathering of open-minded youth welcoming of diverse perspectives and critical thinking."[22] One of the group's goals for the coming year is to improve in the area of "creating opportunities for 'Dialogue Across Culture/Creed' through interfaith youth group opportunities and working with other churches, synagogues, mosques, etc."[23]

Another large Congregational church in the Seattle area has a well-developed sense of identity. They describe themselves as "An open and affirming congregation, we celebrate our diversity in religious background, sexual orientation, race, and abilities."[24]

Their youth pastor, Margaret, like her counterpart in Illinois, has a clear calling to ministry with students and seeks in a variety of ways to help young people feel empowered and to see how God fits into everyday-life issues they face. Her ministry vision statement is: "Youth Group is a place where we TALK about things that matter, we DO things that matter and we KNOW we BELONG! We Build Community through play, service, leadership, celebration, trust and prayer."[25]

Margaret explained to me that very few of her youth group students' friends identify themselves as Christians. They either belong to another religion or have none at all. So they are often in relationship and conversation with a diverse group of young people. Her church affirms itself as wholeheartedly Christian, while acknowledging and celebrating other religions and paths to God. They acknowledge that the congregation comprises many spiritual journeys. Because of this Margaret's model for youth ministry is to affirm the youths' questions and each individual faith journey. While teaching the stories of Jesus and the importance of what he modeled in service, caring for one another, unconditional love and deep justice, she encourages the young people to make their own informed decisions about faith. Her church and youth group seek to embody an extravagant welcome, and by engaging the youth in living out that extravagant welcome, they are invited into the radical message of the gospel characterized by love, justice and restoration of creation. She emphasizes in her ministry that God loves *everyone* and therefore all are welcome.[26]

Certainly there are many commonalities between the youth ministry at the church I attend and that of the Congregational churches in Illinois and Washington. In each case the youth leaders, both professional and volunteer, love youth, love God and sense their call to minister to youth. Both programs balance fun and teaching with serving others. The difference comes, however, in the interpretation of Scripture.

Those who hold the modern view of religious pluralism may affirm the truth of all the verses the traditionalists hold; however, they would add a "but" or a caveat to these verses. For example,

The Spirit of God has been revealed in many places throughout history and it makes no sense (it is in fact, arrogant) to disclaim the truth of other religions and how God, through his Spirit, has revealed himself. Think of religion as a mountain, with knowing God as the peak, and different religions represent different approaches to the peak, all heading toward the same ultimate goal.[27]

This "all heading for the same ultimate goal" is exemplified in the following seminary course description:

This course will explore theological questions posed by religious plurality, especially the diversity among Jews, Christians, and Muslims. If God is One, how can different understandings of that Oneness be valid? Could the One Lord of nature and history have chosen to covenant with different faith communities? And if different communities are, in fact, "chosen" by God through Divine election and revelation, can they come to see themselves as spiritual allies, rather than adversarial rivals for God's favor? Finally, how would a multiplicity of covenants enhance the prospects for the "messianic" transformation of history that our various traditions anticipate? On three occasions, guest teacher/facilitators will be invited to address these questions, drawing on perspectives from Judaism, Christianity, and Islam.[28]

Much of the modern viewpoint of religious pluralism rests on the writings of John Hick.[29] Hick was a conservative Christian until he moved to the United Kingdom to teach philosophy at the University of Birmingham and became closely acquainted with Muslims and Hindus. Hick believes the traditional view of God and Christ is simply not adequate for the modern world and that those who believe in absolute truth must demythologize their own religious singular truth claims.

He seeks to explain four realities that became apparent as his life intersected those of other faith communities.

1. People are religious.

2. Their religious beliefs are not the same.

3. Religious belief is not an illusion.

4. Religion seems to benefit the adherents.[30]

He further rejects naturalism, which holds that all religious truth claims by definition are false. He also rejects religions that see the natural world itself as only illusory.

It seems to Hick, particularly as he observed the religious worship of different faith communities, that they were all seeking an ultimate reality. Call this ultimate reality "God," "Allah," "Spirit" or whatever; it seems to be the same thing. What most religions are after he termed "the Real." Granted, they come at the Real differently, but knowing the Real is the goal. For Hick, embracing religious pluralism is a matter of (1) realizing the common goal of most religions, (2) finding common ground in beliefs about the Real, and (3) discarding exclusivistic or superioristic claims.[31]

Finally, let's consider a third perspective.

POSTMODERN RELIGIOUS PLURALISM

The essence of postmodernism is the notion that beliefs are just that, and that absolute truth is illusory. Truth is "personal" and if you seek to impose your truth upon me you are trying to colonize my life world. Life-world colonization is both arrogant and inappropriate.[32]

One religious denomination that is almost by definition postmodern is the Unitarian Universalist Church. In the Blue Boat blog, a trove of interesting stories about UUC churches or church members, the UUC is described as "a group of people who believe in organized religion but are skeptical about doctrine."[33]

They have extensive resources for youth work and youth ministry leadership infrastructure at a national, regional and congregational level. The Welcome website explains it this way:

> As Unitarian Universalists, our call to the work of youth ministry rests on our spiritual commitment to build the world we dream about—a world in which our faith communities welcome people of all ages, cultures, and backgrounds to join hands in nourishing our spirits and healing the world.
> —The Youth Ministry Working Group Report, 2009.[34]

This is very much in the spirit of Mark Heim, who says that people should not worry about religious doctrines but focus on meeting the real needs of people or as the UUC statement says, "healing the world." Another way to see the priority of UUC youth ministry is to view the curriculum they desire all local youth groups to affirm. Their core teaching curriculum for high school students is called *Tapestry of Faith*. The following is the course description for "A Place for Wholeness":

> Youth, like adults and children, need to be able to talk about what it means to be Unitarian Universalist. Whether delivering an "elevator speech," taking part in an interfaith dialogue, or conversing with friends at the lunch table, youth need practice in describing our multifaceted faith in terms that are personally meaningful and true. Building upon the faith development of Coming of Age and other UU identity programs, this curriculum encourages youth to look inward for a clearer understanding of their personal faith and guides them to express that faith outward into the world.[35]

Another comfortable home for a postmodern view of faith is the Inter-Faith Youth Core, founded by Eboo Patel. This organization, now international in scope, seeks to harness the altruistic DNA of religious youth toward the high calling of helping people in real need. Patel carefully exclaims he is respectful of religious identity; he seeks to unite youth of any or no religious belief for understanding and cooperation.[36] Here the emphasis is not so much about finding common ground religiously. Instead religiousness is seen as unimportant compared to the mighty effort to help the world, help hurting people and become a better person. Postmodern religious pluralists do not expend energy worrying about differing beliefs or understanding theologies.

Postmodern religious pluralism stands on the shoulders of Mark Heim and John Cobb. In *Salvations: Truth and Difference in Religion* Heim acknowledges that every religion has its own exclusivist claims. Nevertheless, there is no one way to salvation; there are, instead *salvations*. Religious people should not worry about these different salvations, instead they should be secure in their own belief or lack thereof.[37] John Cobb extends the implication of this perspective in his *Transforming Christianity and the World*.[38]

In essence Cobb states we are to focus on a "creative response to the world crises.... [We need] passion for the earth and its poor and oppressed people."[39] While Cobb is himself a practicing Christian, his book posits that all doctrines are a response to a particular problem, question or challenge. The Christian faith then is a living faith in that it must now vigorously respond to the world crises. Faith is not important per se, but the response that we and others make is.

SUMMARY

In this chapter we have looked at youth groups representing three different stances toward religious pluralism. We also examined the philosophical underpinnings of each. It's obvious that one's perspective on pluralism (one's theology, actually) affects youth ministry praxis. I have documented this point anecdotally and by scholarly research.

Some may ask, So what? Does it really make any difference in the real world when a youth group is traditional, modern or postmodern?

6

MULTIFAITH PERSPECTIVES: A REASON TO CARE

Youth Religiosity, Flourishing and the Public Good

Though you'll not see this answer posed on the TV game show *Jeopardy!* try your hand at this one:

Answer: This European country's leaders became so concerned about the terrible mindset and behaviors of their teenagers that they mandated an hour of Christian worship or biblical teaching every day in every classroom in the entire country.

I'll give you some help (choose one question):

____ What is Belgium?

____ What is Portugal?

____ What is the United Kingdom?

____ What is Slovenia?

Beginning in the late 1960s and continuing into the 1980s it became almost a universal feeling in this country that their teenagers were, well, *lost*. Purposelessness and despair were the norm, and substance abuse was continuing to rise, and with that criminality.[1]

In the 1980s sociologists from several universities of this country surveyed young people regarding all aspects of their lives and behavior. The effects of income, education, family structure, race, gender and many other possible variables were statistically removed. The researchers were trying to get down to the basic variable or variables that actually made a difference in the lives of youth. What correlates, in a statistically significant way, with prosocial behavior in the youth of that country?

The results were shocking, even to unbiased sociologists. One variable made more difference than any other—by far. Christian faith! And what is the country? The United Kingdom.

RELIGIOSITY AND FLOURISHING YOUTH ARE STRONGLY LINKED

In this UK research, youth who possessed a vital Christian faith possessed a cluster of prosocial behavioral and attitudinal dispositions. There was a linear, statistically significant correlation with religiosity and a flourishing life. This faith-prosocial behavior linkage persisted across the categories of race, class, gender and political geography.[2]

Sociologists measure the religious faith of young people in a variety of ways—worship and youth group attendance, reading Scripture, prayer and other indicators of spiritual engagement. These many measures can be combined into a "group score" of sorts and is termed *religiosity*. Some researchers in the United Kingdom quipped, "Our country either needs to build more prisons, because that's where our youth are going, or we need to find a way to better support Christianity among young people."

The Education Act of 1988 declared that every school in the United Kingdom (England, Scotland, Wales and Northern Ireland) would have regular worship experiences and daily religious education. Religious education became part of the core curriculum along with math, science and history.[3] It had been on the books since 1944, but in 1988 it became *very* important.

It is a fascinating story, especially to any who may be interested in the history of youth ministry.

This requirement for schools to teach religion, however, was very difficult to put into practice at the local level because so few teachers were practicing Christians. In some schools the administration simply parceled out religious education responsibilities to various teachers, who produced materials based on their own knowledge of religion, which apparently included Wicca, Celtic traditional religion, Druidism, Hinduism and others. The Education Act was strengthened in 1994 to specify that the Christian faith was to be taught. At this new Parliamentary directive, many school administrators threw up their hands in despair, and wondered, *Is there anyone we could get to do this for us? Do churches, for example, have youth workers who could come in and relieve us of this burden?*

Prior to 1994 there were probably only a couple hundred full-time youth pastors in the entire United Kingdom. A few years later there were thousands of them, virtually all of whom do "schools work." That is, they go to public schools and hold worship and Bible teaching assemblies or teach in specific classes. A massive infrastructure emerged in the United Kingdom to support youth pastors doing schools work. Christian colleges now offer youth-work degrees. There are training conferences, seminars and excellent Web resources (such as schoolswork.co.uk). Those of us in youth ministry in the United States, where it is almost *illegal* for us to put one foot on a public school campus, fantasize about being welcome at our local high school to teach about the faith and encourage young people to pay attention to this aspect of their lives.

The research findings from the United Kingdom were published in several premier social science journals, and soon sociologists around the globe were asking, "So, there is a correlation between religiosity and prosocial behavior in the United Kingdom. I wonder if the same is true here?"

Yes.

In almost every country on every continent the results are virtually the same: Christian youths who pray often, read the Bible, have a sense of Christ's presence daily, go to youth group, go to church and youth retreats, have characteristics, variously called assets or protective effects, in greater measure than do their less religious peers.

This connects to our previous discussion on pluralism; youth ministry done from a traditional Christian perspective is often more focused on personal religiosity than modernist or postmodernist youth ministries. In chapter five we saw that one's theological point of view affects youth ministry praxis. One example in the National Study of Youth and Religion revealed that there are vast denominationally based differences in youth religiosity.

Why should we care? What does it matter whether we have traditional, modern or postmodern youth ministries? If we care about youth flourishing, it matters a great deal.

We will review a bit of a large trove of data related to youth religiosity and prosocial behavior as well as research that demonstrates religious youth groups make a practical difference. Then we will look at data that shows theologically traditional churches produce highly religious youth with a vital Christian faith.

A bit like C. S. Lewis's conversion. It is well known that C. S. Lewis, an atheist professor at Oxford University, describes his conversion to theism and ultimately to Christianity with the words, "I gave in, and admitted that God was God, and knelt and prayed: perhaps, that night, the most reluctant convert in all England."[4]

In my university days it was not uncommon for professors to rail against the Christian faith. Sociology professors, beholden to Karl Marx's atheism, especially saw no place for Christianity (or any religion) in the academy. Those days are gone now. Those professors who were at their prime in the 1960s and 1970s are now retired.

Peter Berger, a well-known sociologist, claimed in 1967 that Christianity was unimportant now and would fade away to near extinction due to the relentless pressure of modernity.[5] He publicly recanted his unbelief at a major gathering of sociologists in 1999, essentially acknowledging that the religiosity-prosocial behavior link was established and that honest sociologists better wake up to reality. Rodney Stark, another high-profile scholar, said to me in a personal interview, "Whereas fifteen years ago it was rare to find a sociologist in an American university who took religion seriously, today the opposite is the case. One hardly finds a sociologist who does *not* take religion seriously now, though their new respect is sometimes grudging."[6]

Most universities now, unlike thirty years ago, offer multiple courses on religion and, ironically, sociologists have "found religion." And what they've found is that religion makes a difference in the lives of youth.[7]

PROSOCIAL BEHAVIOR AND THE YOUTH-RELIGIOSITY LINK

How is prosocial behavior defined, scaled and measured? In youth religiosity research, prosocial behavior is *the absence of something negative or the presence of something positive for the individual.* The National Study of Youth and Religion was akin to the major study in the United Kingdom done a decade earlier. The NSYR included a literature review of five hundred US-based studies linking high youth religiosity to, for example, low usage of illegal drugs or high incidence of altruistic volunteerism. The NSYR, with the individual as the unit of analysis, involved interviews with over three thousand adolescents nationwide. Nine variable sets with over two hundred variables were quantified. Representative variable sets and variables included

1. Risk behaviors and getting into trouble
   - alcohol consumption
   - smoking
   - cutting class
2. Media consumption
   - weekday TV viewing
   - Internet pornography
   - X-rated movie viewing
3. Sexual activity
   - oral sex
   - sexual intercourse
   - number of sexual partners
4. Emotional well-being
   - feelings about one's own body
   - sadness or depression
   - feeling cared for
5. Connection to adults
   - feelings of being cared for by nonparental adults
   - comfort in speaking with adults
   - number of after school hours without adult supervision.

Each of the two hundred-plus variables measured in the NSYR study is buttressed at a research and conceptual level by studies in the literature that establish the individual asset–individual life outcome link. The following are five examples of variables and how the religiosity link affects behavior and personal outcomes in individual young people.

Youth religiosity and premarital sex. Adolescent premarital sex is a precursor to sexually transmitted diseases, including AIDS, and it is also clearly (and causally) connected to the plight of unwed welfare-dependent teenage mothers. The costs are financial, emotional and quite frequently generational. There is a consistent and statistically significant inverse relationship between adolescent religiosity and premarital sexual experience. For example, in the United States various studies stemming from the National Longitudinal Survey of Youth show this inverse link. Sam Hardy and Marcela Raffaelli sampled white, black and Hispanic youth, and showed that the higher the religiosity, the longer the delay in first sexual experience.[8] Looking at the data yet another way, James Nonnemaker, Clea Mc-Neely and Robert Blum confirmed the now decades-long string of studies that the higher the religiosity of youth the lower likelihood their having ever had intercourse.[9] In a study of Mexican American youth in Texas, religiosity was seen as the best predictor of whether the youth in their 413 student sample were sexually active at the present or ever.[10] A major comparative analysis of ten longitudinal studies regarding youth religiosity and sexual behavior found a consistent inverse correlation with religiosity and female premarital sex in all ten studies. The picture was less clear for adolescent males.[11] Among the most recent studies (2011) is a longitudinal study among teenage virgins that again affirmed that religiosity was associated with the delay in genital touching, oral sex and coitus.[12]

Does high religiosity mean lower premarital sexual activity outside the United States? A study among late-teenage youth in Australia and South Africa had similar results as US studies.[13] Another study, this time among black South African youth only, showed significantly less sexual activity among youth who were high in religiosity.[14]

Is youth religiosity important? Insofar as it reduces teenage premarital sex, the answer is clearly yes. The same is true when it comes to substance abuse.

Youth religiosity and substance abuse. The high social cost of drunk and drugged teenagers is evident almost daily in the popular press. The deleterious impact of smoking on health is well established. The use of these controlled substances by teenagers is seen as a problem by governments and schools. Since this is a high-profile issue, social scientists have engaged in a variety of studies with religiosity as one or more of the independent variables with either direct or indirect effects on youth alcohol, drug and tobacco use.

Researches have given great attention to the urban African American youth population. In a sample of 2,300 urban, poor, black youth, the more they attended church and youth group, the less likely they were to experiment or become controlled-substance users.[15] This correlation held true not only for the younger youth (ages 9-10) but the older youth (ages 18-19) as well. In a similar vein Sung Juon Jang, Bryon Johnson, David Larson and Spencer De'Li found that the power of religious faith and involvement grew throughout adolescence. That is, religious young people in the urban core of US cities were less likely to use illicit drugs, and the older the religious young person, the less likely he or she use controlled substances.[16] In a much earlier study, Stephen Burket explored the direct and indirect effects of parents' religiosity compared to the religiosity of the adolescent. What would be the strongest factor keeping a young person from alcohol abuse? The religiosity of the teenager was most important, whereas the religiosity of the parents had only an indirect effect and a diminishing one at that.[17]

In the social sciences a meta-analysis is a study of other studies. An example of a very ambitious meta-analysis published in *Psychological Reports* looked at twenty-two major studies that all came to the same basic conclusion: in young people the higher the religiosity, the higher the "protective effect" when it came to controlled substances: alcohol, cigarettes, marijuana and other illegal drugs. That is, youth with a highly active and real faith were less likely to experiment with or become a user of these controlled substances.[18]

In the United Kingdom, Ian Sutherland and John Shepherd looked at a host of substance abuse issues with 451 eleven- to sixteen-year-olds from five schools. Religiosity was correlated negatively with substance abuse, and the effect became more pronounced the older the youth.[19] Similar results were shown in former communist-block Hungary, where outward forms of religiosity were illegal up until 1989. In a study of 1,240 youth in Szeged, high religiosity meant lower substance abuse.[20]

Youth religiosity and social bonding and attachment. Social bonding and attachment are closely linked to youth flourishing. Youth groups serve as venues for social bonding. Many youth groups provide a dizzying array of subgroups to take part in. There might be Sunday school, a weekly small group ministry, a discipleship/accountability group, a basketball team, a worship band, a drama ministry or worship dance team. In religious youth groups the potential for peer disapproval of negative behavior is very high. Peer disapproval is another way to express the concept of Émile Durkheim's "attachment to groups" or the notion of the social bond.[21] Durkheim's description of morality is germane to student ministry praxis and understanding the theoretical link between belief, bonding and behavior. For Durkheim morality does not exist within an individual unless he or she feels strong attachment to a group (or groups). The person must carry in his or her mind a collection of social facts. Social facts are recurrent aspects of human behavior that provide an ordered framework or set of rules in which people function. A social fact is external. It is outside and independent of the individual.

Second, morality is "constraining in character"; that is, a person aware of a certain social fact would feel a sense of wrongdoing should the fact be ignored. Attachment to the group means the person will not act in a way that will damage or hurt the social group. This attachment, in normative socialization, begins with the family and expands to school, other groups (like a religious youth group) and eventually society. The person who is aware of what a group expects and is committed to avoid violating, displeasing or confusing others within the social group will behave in a moral fashion vis-à-vis that social group. When a person is not properly attached to a group, that is, he or she lacks awareness of social facts, this person is likely to behave in a manner that the group sees as wrong. Attachment and social bonding has proven to be a huge and fertile field for sociologists. Social bonding correlates positively with behavior that is good for society, and more recently it has been shown to correlate positively with youth religiosity.

Social bonding is a personal feeling of connectedness to peers, family, school, a common interest group or community. Andrew Cherry studied junior high school students in one Delaware town and found that the more connected kids felt to the school and its groups, the more socially constructive their behavior.[22] Another study involving one thousand junior high students in Rochester, New York, found that attachment to parents, school and teachers was a significant determinant of decreased at-risk behavior compared to young people who were not so well attached to others.[23] The greater the attachment, the less delinquency and drug use. These findings support a 1992 study in Ohio that also tested the association of attachment to school and teachers with delinquent behaviors.[24] Higher religiosity correlated with higher social bonding (and lower delinquency) in a major study by Johnson, Jang, Larson and De'Li.[25]

Adolescent bonding with parents is strongly correlated with academic success, and a host of studies demonstrate that youth high in religiosity are more likely to have healthy bonding with their parents. For example, in Sweden a study of 196 youth showed that religiously active youth were more bonded to their parents than their secular peers.[26] Similar results were found in the urban context of the United States.[27]

Another study of 2,300 teenagers randomly selected in a national sample found that youth religiosity spilled over into school activity participation rates. For example, kids highly active in church were more involved in school clubs (83%) than their church inactive peers (44%), their school sports participation was slightly higher (67% to 63%), school music participation more than twice as high (75% to 34%) and so was their involvement in other school activities (49% to 30%). Highly religious kids were much more likely to do more than six hours homework per week (69% to 47%).

Youth religiosity and emotional and mental health. Who doesn't want to see young people experience a positive sense of self, be empowered and have the ability to get over the normal setbacks and crises that are part of teenage life? Youth religiosity is highly and positively associated with resilience in adolescents.

One meta-analysis of US-based research revealed a convergence of similar results correlating a vital religious life with outcomes such as purpose in life, the ability to forgive and to move on, and a sense of well-being. Mental health professionals show a keen interest in such research. One does not have to work long in adolescent social services, counseling or adolescent psychiatric wards to wonder why some kids are so troubled while others seem to face similar life setbacks without much difficulty. In nonscholarly terms, youths with a vital faith have something their less-religious peers do not possess.[28]

As with other youth religiosity research the results are similar around the globe. The following abstract from a recently published study in the United Kingdom is typical.

Most studies show that religion is a protective factor for **mental health**. A few argue that it is detrimental and the remainder conclude it makes no difference. We investigate the **religiosity** correlates of childhood psychopathology—strength of belief, importance of being able to practice one's religion, and worship frequency. Questions on **religiosity** were included in the **mental health** survey of children in Great Britain administered to 2992 11-19 year-olds in 2007. The Development and Well-Being Assessment was used to generate rates of clinically recognizable **mental** disorders. Logistic regression analysis was used to establish the magnitude of the **religiosity** correlates of **emotional** and conduct disorders. Young people with a stated religion who had weakly held beliefs or who regarded religious practice as unimportant were those with the greater likelihood of having **emotional** disorders. Regular attendance at religious services or prayer meetings reduced the likelihood of having a conduct disorder.[29]

In São Paulo, Brazil, an interesting study was conducted among 325 incarcerated teenagers. The research involved first assessing their exposure to community violence, such as a neighbor, friend, sibling or parent being the victims of beating, torture, or murder. They then surveyed religiosity, focusing on both the interior sense of God in prayer and their past exterior participation in organized religious expression (worship). Finally, each young person was given an extensive mental health survey and interview. They concluded, "religiosity may indeed buffer the relation between violence exposure and certain mental health problems."[30]

Youth religiosity and personal morality/moral reasoning. We have reviewed a tiny slice of social science research regarding adolescent religiosity and its behavioral and attitudinal outcomes. Aspects of the research we have looked at measure the evidence of personal morality and moral reasoning (e.g., sexual behavior, drug usage). Yet another category of social science research seeks to measure adolescent *moral reasoning* itself and how this moral reasoning (or lack thereof) affects behavior.

Though there is not a vast literature *proving* that church youth groups produce personal morality and moral reasoning in young people, we can confidently proceed for several reasons. First, we know that from the previously cited studies, personal morality is a component of religiosity and makes a difference in behavior. Second, church youth groups teach and model personal morality. Whether the youth leaders are coming from a traditional, modern or postmodern perspective, we can assume that personal morality is modeled and either latently or explicitly taught. Third, fostering personal morality is an explicitly stated goal of many denominational youth ministries.[31]

Lawrence Kohlberg's famous work regarding moral development began in the late 1960s and continued through the 1980s.[32] Morality, according to Kohlberg, develops at three levels, each with two stages. While many are familiar with the Kohlberg's stages, a key point critical to the "good for society" discussion should not be overlooked. He believes there is a positive benefit for society as more people ascend the stages of moral reasoning. His research reveals what triggers moral growth:"The more social settings encourage role taking, voluntary participation, communication, and decision making, the more individuals confronted with these settings will advance to higher stages of moral consciousness."[33]

This is *exactly* what many youth groups do. They are young people doing what they do best: socialize with their peers. Youth groups are social settings par excellence. Decision making is central. Participation is voluntary. While "parental constraint" may account for the presence of a young person in Sunday school, kids participate in religious youth groups because they want to. And communication—adult to youth, youth to youth and youth to adult—is central. This communication is often about spiritual matters, but as often it is about life-world experiences played out on the stage of daily life.

In chapter five we saw that those youth pastors who eschewed infant baptism were much more likely to have some kind of youth leadership structure in which young people are empowered to make decisions.[34] One large youth ministry (traditional perspective) in New York City, for example, has many extracurricular activities for their kids, including various sports teams, dance groups, bands, choirs, and literary and social service action groups. Most of these are led not by adults but by older youth (ages 18-20). The drama group decides how to best illustrate a point in the youth pastor's pending sermon. The music and dance groups plan how to support the theme of the morning. These kids feel empowered, and younger ones look forward to being able to step into leadership. These activities create strong peer pressure for kingdom-related *aspiration* and *achievement*.

In my judgment, if one were to imagine an ideal type of social setting to move a young person from one moral stage to the next, it would be difficult to envision anything better than the religious youth group.

We have reviewed literature that reveals there are positive behavioral, health and dispositional outcomes associated the vital faith. Youth groups contribute both to personal religiosity and attachment and moral reasoning. These outcomes contribute to the public good. Youth workers can be doubly thankful: their work is good for the kingdom and for their community.

DENOMINATIONAL DIFFERENCES IN ADOLESCENT
VITAL FAITH CREATION

The National Study of Youth and Religion asked students questions about their personal religiosity that provide a nuanced understanding of their interior spirituality (see table 6.1). Some questions asked reveal that conservative Protestant youth were higher in religious experience and expression. Mainline Protestant youth were stronger in some areas. Generally, Roman Catholic youth were some distance behind their Protestant peers.

Table 6.1. Personal Religious Practices, US Adolescents, Ages 13 to 17

In the past year, the teen has	US	CP	MP	RC
practiced spiritual meditation not including prayer	10%	8%	10%	10%
been part of a prayer, or Bible group at school	15%	25%	17%	8%
taught Sunday school or its equivalent	20%	28%	26%	15%
burned candle or incense that had spiritual meaning	21%	14%	24%	35%
fasted as a spiritual discipline	24%	22%	25%	29%
been part of any other Bible or prayer group	27%	42%	31%	17%
played or sang in a Christian youth band or youth choir	28%	37%	35%	18%
read a devotional or spiritual book other than Bible	30%	45%	28%	22%
spoken publicly about their faith	30%	42%	33%	20%
attended a religious music concert	34%	51%	51%	20%
shared their faith with someone not of their faith	43%	56%	51%	37%
listened to Christian music (any media)	51%	70%	52%	35%
worked hard to reconcile a broken relationship	59%	61%	63%	61%
prays alone at least once a day, often more	38%	49%	32%	33%

(US = all US youth, CP = conservative Protestants, MP = mainline Protestants, RC = Roman Catholic)

Source: Adapted from Christian Smith and Melinda Denton, *Soul Searching: The Religious and Spiritual Lives of American Teenagers* (New York: Oxford University Press, 2005), p. 46.

The following Protestant denominations had high enough participation numbers for researchers to be able to make statistically significant comparisons: Assemblies of God (AG), Disciples of Christ

Table 6.2. Percent of Youth, by Denomination, Feeling Very or Extremely Close to God Most of the Time

Assemblies of God	53
Disciples of Christ	38
Evangelical Covenant	22
Evangelical Lutheran	43
Lutheran Church—Missouri Synod	48
Presbyterian Church USA	45
Southern Baptist Convention	49
United Methodist	38
black Baptist	55
Church of God in Christ	48
conservative Protestant	46
mainline Protestant	36
black Protestant	48
all Protestant	44
all teenagers	38

Table 6.3. Percent of Youth, by Denomination, in Which Faith Is Very or Extremely Important in Shaping Daily Life

Assemblies of God	77
Disciples of Christ	47
Evangelical Covenant	40
Evangelical Lutheran	61
Lutheran Church—Missouri Synod	54
Presbyterian Church USA	55
Southern Baptist Convention	72
United Methodist	45
black Baptist	76
Church of God in Christ	91
conservative Protestant	64
mainline Protestant	43
black Protestant	69
all Protestant	60
all teenagers	51

(DC), Episcopal Church USA (ECUSA), Evangelical Lutheran Church of America (ELCA), Lutheran Church—Missouri Synod (LCMS), Presbyterian Church USA (PCUSA), Southern Baptist Convention (SBC), United Methodist Church (UMC), black Baptists (BB, 3 denoms.), Church of God in Christ (COGIC). Table 6.2 reveals that denominations whose youth ministry praxis leans traditional tend to produce young people with a higher sense of vital faith.[35]

It is interesting to note that the more conservative of the Lutheran denominations (LCMS) has slightly higher results than its less conservative counterpart (ELCA). The Episcopal Church lags behind all the other denominations in the "sense of God's closeness" category.

When it comes to faith being very or extremely important in daily life, we see in table 6.3 that more than 50 percent of the youth in all the conservative churches indicated this was true in their lives. Mainline churches were less strong in this regard.

Another way to capture a sense of the interiority of adolescent spiritual life is their response to whether they experience answered prayer and a sense of direct guidance from God (see table 6.4).

Once again real differences are apparent. Fifty percent or more of the youth of some mainline and all conservative denominations sense God's guidance and answered prayer. The Episcopal church young people, however, lag in this regard.

Table 6.4. Answered Prayer or Direct Guidance from God

Assemblies of God	57
Disciples of Christ	44
Evangelical Covenant	32
Evangelical Lutheran	56
Lutheran Church—Missouri Synod	46
Presbyterian Church USA	59
Southern Baptist Convention	66
United Methodist	49
black Baptist	76
Church of God in Christ	55
conservative Protestant	65
mainline Protestant	46
black Protestant	60
all Protestant	59
all teenagers	51

SUMMARY

In this chapter we saw that sociologists have established a correlation between youth religiosity and positive behaviors and mental health. These outcomes not only have personal significance but are important to a community. Youth religiosity research also shows a disparity among denominations in this regard. Conservative denominations and churches tend to produce more highly religious youth.

Regardless of our denominational ties, we all want to see youth flourish spiritually. Chapter seven will examine how we can facilitate a vital Christian identity among students.

YOUTH MINISTRY AMONG NONES AND FUNCTIONAL SYNCRETISTS

Mission Possible 1

Individuals become nones in at least four distinct ways. Therefore one approach won't work with all types. In this chapter we will work with the four-context descriptions I have supplied in chapter three. For each type, I will share my own approach as well as resources and approaches of others.

FAMILY CONTEXT NONES

Family context nones come from a family background in which religion and faith are not modeled or discussed. They are likely neither hostile or skeptical, but carry an awareness that some people are religious, whatever that may mean.

How and why do these nones end up in our youth group meetings and programs? It's not because of slick advertising but because they were invited *by* and come *with* a friend. We have members of our youth group name five of their "most wanted" friends so we can pray for them. We pray that they would visit our youth group and come to faith. Our youth group meetings certainly are for the spiritual growth and encouragement of Christian students, but they also are understandable and accessible to nones.

These meeting are designed to help nones be open to the gospel, become part of the group and then realize that faith has sprouted in their hearts. They then are ready to self-identify as followers of Christ. What program features help this happen?

Certainly, worship is an important element. Seeing peers engaged with something (Someone) beyond themselves may trigger a feeling of wonder or curiosity. I have participated in some European youth festivals that bring together nones and Christian teenagers.[1] Often events like these are the first time students from Eastern Europe, whose parents were atheists *by law* under communism, encounter a person their age who is a practicing Christian. It is astonishing, unexpected and filled with mystery. Many of them want to know how they can have what these Christian peers have.

Though the none students who have shown up in my youth groups were not from former communist countries, their stereotypes of religion and religious people often are disrupted by what they see and feel in the group.

I confess, music has never been my strength as a youth worker. Not only am I not musical but I'm not very good at recruiting musical people. There have been rare exceptions, but they have been just that, exceptions to my norm of zero music in my youth group meetings. In spite of this sad fact, none students have often come to Christ via the youth group meetings I've had a part in.

One thing that interests them is a student-led youth ministry. I try to get kids to lead any way I can. And when I lead a typical twenty- to thrity-minute Bible lesson, I *never* speak more than seven minutes, often less. I have students leading pieces of the lesson, and much time is spent in processing the lesson and in small group discussion.[2] A paradigm shift often occurs to none students who experience a youth ministry with a high percentage of student leadership. They see peers who love Christ, and over time what once was inconceivable becomes imaginable, even possible and sometimes *desirable*. I have seen this happen hundreds of times. Student leadership paired with peer-to-peer care and love becomes a compelling apologetic to nones. My student leadership core (see chap. 8) creates a climate of friendship, openness and care. When a none first comes to the youth group, he or she is a little disoriented by the vibe of this group compared to school. As the none continues to come, he or she begins to belong and eventually begins to believe.

A good example of a youth leader training resource and curriculum that emphasizes student-to-student care is Sonlife (sonlife .com). They anchor their whole ministry perspective on the model of Jesus' ministry in the Gospels. Jesus modeled care to his disciples. How do we do that and help our students do it too? The tools we use to create care includes retreats, small groups, service projects and Bible teaching that facilitates an "other centered" consciousness.

How do we help none parents?

I find that some none parents are open to me as a Christian youth worker and don't mind that their son or daughter is becoming interested in a Christian youth group.

Sometimes *single parents* feel desperate, especially single mothers of boys.[3] If our student ministry actively engages the adolescent son or daughter in what are deemed "positive activities," the religious content is often seen as innocuous or irrelevant to a grateful parent. To have caring adults and seemingly "together" peers actively caring about a son or daughter helps the single parent feel she or he is not alone. Being cognizant of the financial pressures many single parents experience and the potentially prohibitive costs of some youth group events, retreats or trips, I offer these teens a 50 percent subsidy or more if necessary.[4]

None parents who are in some kind of crisis or under chronic stress seem wide open to their son's or daughter's involvement in a Christian youth group. I find that stressed parents feel guilty they are not providing for their children as well as they would like. They do not have the time or energy to help their son or daughter get involved in fun activities or extracurricular events that would add value to his or her life. A student ministry that provides their daughter or son with friendship, transportation, financial help (when needed), new experiences and the chance to learn new skills can be pretty impressive to stressed-out parents.

BEHAVIORAL PREFERENCE NONES

Behavioral preference nones perceive that religion will suppress their ability or desire to party, act out or be sexually active. These students typically do not show up in our youth group meetings to check things out. Instead, they avoid anything to do with religion.

In four decades of student ministry leadership I have seen only one path (with two subsequent branches) that may lead a behavioral preference none to faith: the proximity of a peer, a friend, who is a Christian of living faith.

The none student may understand this friend is religious, even Christian, and respond that it is "her choice" or "It's fine for him; that's cool, but it's not for me" or "Whatever works, just don't push it on me." Nevertheless, knowing a practicing Christian peer (who also cares about his or her friends spiritually) is the first step. There are two scenarios in which a none who has a Christian friend comes to faith.

The first scenario is that the Christian friend invites this none to something that sounds amazingly fun. I've used Jello wrestling and pudding fights as special events. (It is precisely here that some may heap criticism on Christian youth ministry and its emphasis on fun.) My students find it easy to invite a friend to something like this. My urban youth worker friends use basketball tournaments as a draw.

My artsy and hip youth worker friends have a storefront or warehouse stocked with the latest electronics and media equipment, and have rehearsal space and recording studios (I'm not making this up). And kids, brought by Christian friends, come. I've used retreats or trips to desired destinations as outreach. For example, my Seattle and Vancouver youth group students found it easy to invite friends to ski and snowboard retreats at Whistler, British Columbia. In my New Jersey church I used winter retreat trips to Quebec as an "invite a friend" event.

In the context of fun events or amazing retreats I've seen "noneness" get deconstructed, not through teaching or preaching, but by being with Christian peers and seeing firsthand that one does not have to be drunk, high or in bed to have a great time.

The second scenario that draws a none to Christ is when she or he experiences a crisis that is too hard to handle. The none's parents may be unable to help, or they may be the cause of the crises. A none in crisis, desperately seeking help, may wonder about that one Christian friend, *Can she help me? What does he have that I don't?*

I find that parents of behavioral preference nones are often profoundly grateful for the positive influence a Christian youth group has on their wayward son or daughter.

INTELLECTUAL ISSUES WITH CHRISTIANITY NONES

Nones that have intellectual issues with Christianity do not normally show up at youth group when invited, and they may even resist the urge to ski at Whistler or some other high-profile youth program. They steer clear of Christian youth events because they assume they will be preached at. They want none of it.

On occasion I have met these students when one is with a youth group member at a coffee, ice cream or a burger shop. I get introduced, and the none's eyes reflect his or her thoughts: *Poor stupid soul.*

I know my friend here thinks this guy is great, but how can he be so dumb? Sometimes they'll smile and fire a question or two at me—something like "So, can God make something so heavy he can't pick it up?" Or perhaps, "Since you believe God makes everything, does he make babies that have severe birth defects?" Or "So you believe that just because someone is born in Mongolia and they've never heard of Jesus, they will go to hell when they die?" I'm sometimes told that these nones later comment to my youth group student, "Well, I guess he's not as dumb as I thought."[5]

The only way I have seen an intellectual issue none come to faith is through a crisis that the none cannot handle alone. A none in crisis often turns to a Christian friend, and sometimes even to me.

If I were invited to converse with none parents who are likewise skeptical for intellectual reasons, I would first ask how they came to nonfaith. I would then ask them if by chance they had read the French scholar Alain de Botton's book *Religion for Atheists: A Non-Believer's Guide to the Uses of Religion.*[6] As I mentioned earlier, it is a compelling read. De Botton believes that religious faith is nonsense, but that atheists and agnostics should steal the good things that religion creates, such as wisdom, community, kindness, tenderness, educational motivation and perspective.[7] Then I would invite them to consider the corpus of social science religiosity research (see chap. 5), which compellingly shows that living faith causes a host of positive life outcomes in adolescents and young adults. I would also ask them to consider something that may be *an inconvenient truth:* that the relation between living faith and these positive life outcomes is *linear;* that is, the more living faith a young person has, the better off the young person is.[8] If the vibe was right in this conversation I would then comment, "I'm not suggesting you change your stance on faith, but I am suggesting you consider it okay that your son or daughter explores religious faith. Apparently, a great deal depends on it."

NEGATIVE EXPERIENCE NONE

We must admit that since Christians are indeed human, there is, unfortunately, ample opportunity for persons, young and old, to have a negative experience with Christians or in the church. The sad thing is, of course, that the rest of us get painted with that same negative brush. I cringe when I recall the negative encounters some students in my own youth ministries have experienced. I recall Anne, the rather attractive eleventh grader who appeared in our youth group when her family had moved to the area. The boys were noticing her (an understatement!). On her second visit to our youth group meeting I was cleaning up the food table at the end of the meeting and overhead behind me one of our most discipled and leadership-oriented girls, a senior, say to Anne, "We don't need you here."⁹ Or I think of Charlie, cognitively and physically disabled, who was so proud of the huge watermelon he brought to our youth group. During our "Summer Study and Swim Series" we always met at a home with a swimming pool. Cruelly, two of our other regular attenders (both males) took the watermelon from Charlie and smashed it on the road in front of the house where we were meeting, laughing at both Charlie's shock and the hipness of their action.

Sigh! Times like these cause me to wonder if a career at Home Depot or Walmart might be more suitable.

If a negative experience none begins to come to youth group (always at the invitation of a vital-faith friend) and I have found out about his or her background, I don't do anything other than pray. I observe that more often than not the new student seems to enjoy the experience and over time begins to identify with the group, sometimes even coming to faith. In these cases the caring Christian youth community deconstructs noneness through the fruit of the Spirit lived out before the newcomer. It must eventually dawn on the new student that not all Christians (young or old) are mean, hypocritical or abusive.

I've never had the opportunity to personally engage with a parent who is a none due to negative experience. (If I have known such parents, they did not identify themselves as such.) I have observed, however, that almost always nonchurched parents begin to like what they see in their son or daughter as a result of youth group attendance, and they are impressed with the quality of interest and care evidenced by the adults who are part of the student ministry leadership.

STUDENT MINISTRY AMONG THOSE OF À LA CARTE FAITH

I was having one of those nights with our junior high group where everything went right. Well, almost everything. Attendance was good and the games went well. The kids (about forty 11- to 13-year-olds) participated with enthusiasm and did not adopt an "I'm too cool for this" attitude. They sat quietly when I was giving the Bible study, and many hands shot up when I asked discussion questions. My theme was unity and being kind to one another. The main point was, just like the early church, our group is very diverse, yet it can be a safe place. All heads nodded their assent. It was one of those times when, had it been a camp situation, we would have joined hands and sung "Kumbaya" or Michael W. Smith's "Friends Are Friends Forever," with faces and hearts aglow.

When we closed in prayer, over half the kids prayed out loud, variously offering thanksgiving to God for our wonderful group or praying that we would be kind, have unity and so on. It was one of those nights when things went right. Right, that is, until just after the last amen.

Sitting on my left side were the guys. They often tried to act tough, macho and oh-so-cool. The girls were on my right. Two seconds after I said amen and we were all enjoying the moment, Troy yelled, "Hey Liz, you're fat, and you're ugly!" He rolled over in laughter and was joined by most of the other guys in uproarious delight at such a well-timed insult. While the guys were still rolling on the floor, Liz stood to her feet, briefly surveyed the guys who were mocking her, burst into tears and ran from the room.

The rest of the group quickly dispersed as parents arrived to pick up their kids. It didn't take a PhD to figure out what would be reported to parents on the way home.

If this had happened to you, which do you feel would have been the best course of action?

- Confront Troy and banish him from the group for a month as discipline.

- Call a parent meeting to go over acceptable behavior in youth group meetings.

- Call the pastor or elders and report the incident. Perhaps then seek a meeting with Troy and his parents to agree on appropriate discipline.

- None of the above.

- Resign and seek a career with Home Depot or Starbucks.

  I picked "None of the above."

  I confronted Troy kindly in the parking lot. "Troy, I was a little confused by what you did in there. Weren't you one of the people who thanked God for the wonderful feeling and unity we have in this group?" Troy replied, "She's my sister, I can say what I want." "Well Troy, what you did was wrong, and I know you'll feel differently about this eventually." He then turned and got into the car that was waiting to take him and his sister Liz home.

  I didn't worry about the incident or do any follow-up. I knew Troy had yet to receive his cerebral upgrade. (*Cerebral upgrade* is my term for the hormonally triggered wiring of the prefrontal cortex of the brain, from which emanates the ability to think and reason deeply.)

I knew that when Troy got his cerebral upgrade it would finally occur to him that the Christian faith actually applies at home, at school and at youth group meetings, and it is even applicable to siblings. By the time a year had passed and Troy was in ninth grade, he had had his upgrade and was a Christian who evidenced the fruit of the Spirit everywhere, including at home with his sister.

This chapter examines adolescent cognitive development (which has many implications for youth work, including dealing with adolescent misbehavior), and gleaning how the insights gained may help inform our efforts to mitigate the cultural pressure toward syncretism and Moralistic Therapeutic Deism.[10]

THE CEREBRAL UPGRADE

Those who work with teenagers have observed at least two things having to do with cognitive development: (1) young teens are different from older teens when it comes to the ability to "get it," and (2) that girls generally "get it" before boys.

Jean Piaget was among the first to propose a cognitive development schema, calling the maturation that takes place in adolescence "formal operations" or "abstract thinking."[11] One helpful way to think of this is that a child is incapable of thinking about a thought. That is, a child cannot reflect on the fact that he or she is thinking. Sometime between eleven and thirteen for girls and fourteen-plus for boys, hormones complete the wiring of the prefrontal cortex. Neuroscience tells us that the prefrontal cortex is where abstract thinking, time horizon, risk assessment and emotional intelligence emerge in the brain. Additionally, "executive function" and impulse control is generated by the prefrontal cortex.[12]

Another way to illustrate it is that a seven-year-old, for example, can express an opinion about liking their family car (it's red!). But they are not able to explore the meaning of that thought in their head.

They are *not* able to ponder why they like the family car: *Is it the advertising I've seen? Is it that our neighbors have a car like ours? Is it because this car is appropriate to our socioeconomic status?*

When the prefrontal cortex starts to wire-up, it changes nearly everything for the young person. Typically they revisit every major area of their lives, including faith. *Why do I believe in God? What will my future be? Life is full of choices, I can't do everything, which will I choose and why? I want to be distinct from my parents, how can I do that?*[13]

It is quite fun to watch the intellectual lights first come on in student ministry. When it happens the early teen girls are capable of deep spirituality, while the boys would rather play sports or blow stuff up (video games). I also enjoy seeing the slightest evidence that the boys have a prefrontal cortex at all, and over a year or two see them experience the delight, fun and terror of thinking about things in an entirely different way. That is, of course, what I knew would happen to Troy.

There are many theories why it appears that prefrontal cortex development is happening later in life then it did decades ago. The academic consensus is settling around the notion that well-meaning parents are oversheltering their sons and daughters. That is, being too zealous to shield their kids from disappointment, setback, pain and responsibility. For example, in rural America, at least in the past if not the present, children and youth had responsibilities around the farm. Whether it was bringing in the eggs, milking the cows or making sure the horses had water, a farm kids could see the importance of their contribution to the family.[14]

Let's see how understanding the cerebral upgrade may influence how we approach the subject of pluralism.

With younger teens, it is certainly fine to present the beliefs and practices of other religions. It is certainly fine to explain that "of course we know the Bible teaches Jesus is the only way." While perhaps one of the girls may then ask, "Does that mean my Buddhist locker partner is going to hell?" the vast majority of young teen boys will just take our words at face value and not give it a second thought.[15]

With older teens who have had their cerebral upgrade, we have the joy (and maybe the pain) of helping them wrestle with the not-so-subtle implications of the historic Christian faith's view of Jesus as the only way of salvation. We can also give kids experiences and teaching that helps them see how important it is to not go à la carte when it comes to faith. We can model and teach what it means to believe in Christ as the only way, while at the same time be loving and welcoming to our friends of other faiths or no faith at all.

We will come back to this hugely important topic shortly.

CAN ANYTHING BE DONE TO HASTEN COGNITIVE DEVELOPMENT?

It is my observation that cognitive and moral development are closely linked in teenagers, which makes sense. When we are developed enough to understand that we are recipients of God's grace and mercy, it make us grateful and gives us the desire to live a life of gratitude, passing on to others the grace and love that has been given to us.

As stated earlier, cognitive development can be hastened through a rich social environment that includes youth who are empowered to interact, plan and carry out those plans.[16]

Of course a youth group is an ideal venue for group decision making. For nearly four decades I have used a student-leadership-team approach to most youth ministries I have been involved with. That is, I have students in charge of certain major and minor decisions within the student ministry setting. In the context of our leadership team meetings, their ideas are put forward, evaluated, debated and ultimately decided on. The list of opportunities for student decision making are nearly endless: dramas, musicals, mission trips,

Vacation Bible Schools and so on. Educators today would say *critical thinking* is facilitated in collaborative decision making.

Taking responsibility for things that matter is the other side of the coin. Student-led small groups are a good example of youth responsibility. I use students (even young teens) to lead part of the Bible study or a portion of an outreach event. My personal policy is "The more important the event, the more important that youth are leading up front, much of the time if not the whole time."

Another strategy I use to encourage moral and cognitive development is to ask pre-cerebral-upgrade boys about their future behavior or what their behavior would look like if viewed from space.

Marcus was in eighth grade, and by the middle of that year he was almost six feet tall and weighed nearly two hundred pounds. Some of the sixth graders in the group were only chest high to and less than half Marcus's weight. Marcus loved to hog a whole couch to himself after playing group games. He would run into the youth room, jump over the back of a couch and spread himself out to take up all the space. If there was another kid already on the couch, Marcus shoved the kid with his massive foot until the couch was his alone.

Marcus had a good side, however. Sometimes during the Bible study I could tell he was listening, and he occasionally made a comment or asked a question that showed a hint of cerebral activity.

One evening I purposely ran in from outside along with the kids. As usual, Marcus jumped over the back of the couch and splayed himself across it. I sat on the floor, literally at his feet.

"Hey Marcus, got a question for you."

"What's up?"

"How old do you think you'll be when you stop hogging the couch all to yourself?"

"What do you mean?" He looked at me with eyes wide.

"What I mean is that when you get into the high school group next year you'll probably observe that no one behaves the way you do when it comes to couch sitting. They share. Sometimes even boys and girls sit on the same couch. So, I was just curious, what year in high school do you think you might be when you start sharing the couch too?"

Marcus starred at me and eventually offered, "I dunno."

He never hogged the couch again, *ever.*

Here's another example.

Brian had a gift for verbal torture. He was a hyperactive seventh-grader. One of his main activities before and after youth group was to tease, ridicule and humiliate a small sixth-grade girl. Brian projected the image of being cool, urbane, hip, popular and worldly wise. He took every opportunity to help Missy know she was the absolute opposite: stupid, out of it and worthless. I had to hand it to Missy; she seemed generally unfazed by this negative attention. She was a deeply Christian girl (for a sixth-grader, anyway), and although I'm sure she would rather not face Brian's onslaughts each week, she nevertheless came faithfully week after week.

Another youth pastor had already addressed the group about how we treat each other, but Brian either didn't hear or didn't care. I did notice, though, that on rare occasions during Bible study Brian sometimes said something insightful. He had, as it were, one foot on the dock and one foot on the rowboat. Generally he was extremely immature, but there were glimpses of what I hoped would be the mature Christian that would eventually emerge.

One night when Brian's verbal abuse of Missy had risen to new heights, I pulled him aside (not in anger, but it was clear to him that he was to come with me). "Brian, I'm going to give you some feedback. I know you are not asking for any, but I'm going to give you some feedback anyway."

He stared off into space, purposely avoiding my eyes.

"If I was from another planet and was visiting earth for the very first time and was sitting here for the last half hour, I would have concluded that it was your sole purpose as a human being to torture Missy. I would have guessed that this is all you have had on your mind all day, and that tonight, now that you two are in the same place, you are unleashing all the negative things you've been planning against her."

He continued to look away.

"So I guess I'm a little confused. In Bible study sometimes you seem to say that you are a Christian and believe the Bible and stuff. Yet out here, you are clearly trying to make Missy not only miserable but miserable that she was ever born in the first place. So, what gives? Help me understand."

He ran off to join his friends.

Brian did not come near Missy the rest of the evening. He didn't next week either. Missy and her family moved away at the end of the school year, and as far as I observed and know from others, Brian had completely ceased his rotten treatment of her. I think my extraterrestrial point of view got his attention and made him actually try to think about something from a different point of view. Seeing a different point of view is a marker of the beginnings of a cerebral upgrade. Having said that, though, and looking back on it, I probably should have gone further some weeks later and asked him to apologize to Missy when I noticed his behavior had consistently changed for the better. I missed an opportunity to affirm him, which was unfortunate since especially middle school kids don't get much positive adult input.

To me, one of the most enjoyable things about youth work is being on hand to watch kids mature before my very eyes. In Brian's case the next school year he was contributing regularly and positively to the discussion times in Bible study. In high school he was on the student leadership team and admired for his commitment to both the youth group and to Christ.

Whether they become cerebrally upgraded early, late or right on schedule, we can help Christian adolescents be less inclined toward an à la carte faith. Let's look at how several different youth ministries intentionally help their students in this way.

STORIES FROM THE FRONT

How are youth groups today seeking to help their own young people maintain a traditional Christian faith that is vital, heartfelt and welcoming?

To get a feel for what was actually happening in youth groups (aside from the one I volunteer in) I received permission to survey the youth workers of the Evangelical Free Church of America, which comes from the traditional Christian perspective described in chapter five. I appreciated more than a decade earlier their being one of the four Protestant denominations that participated in my PhD research on youth group numerical growth.[17]

The first questions of my survey covered demographic and ministry context matters, while the other questions addressed matters related to "Jesus as the only way." The survey is not scientific in that it is not a random sample of Evangelical Free youth workers. The results cannot be generalized to other conservative youth workers, or youth workers of any denomination. Having said that, seventy of their full-time youth workers completed the survey and returned it to me within twelve hours of the survey launch. Their answers provide an interesting glimpse of how these particular youth pastors conceptualize and experience the subjects of the adolescent tolerance, syncretism and à la carte faith. Some narrated their experiences at considerable length. All the data reflected here speaks of these seventy full-time youth pastors.

Survey summary. The youth workers of the Evangelical Free Church have been serving in their church, that is, the same church, for 6.35 years. That is a year longer than the typical youth pastor stays in his or her post according to other research.[18] Eighty-six percent are male and the middle age range (42%) is thirty to thirty-nine. Two-thirds of these youth workers have a ministry-oriented bachelor's or master's degree and another 25 percent have a bachelor's or master's degree in a different subject area. Just over half minister to youth groups that are combined middle and high school age; most of the others lead groups that are senior high school only.

Survey question 7 reads: "I believe Jesus Christ is the only way of salvation, that only Christianity, no other religions or religious leaders, provide a way for salvation and heaven." They had to choose one of three answers: yes, not sure, not really.

All seventy youth pastors chose yes.

They were then asked to indicate how often Jesus as the one and only way to salvation was addressed in a typical year. Ninety-one percent indicated "We present on this more than once a year." I next

Table 7.1. Youth Ministry Setting Where "Jesus as the One and Only Way" Is Presented

Especially if you teach/present once a year or more, what is the setting?

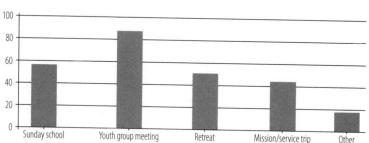

asked what youth ministry settings this teaching took place in. Table 7.1 presents the results.

Survey question 11 stated, "If you teach on this once or more a year, describe how you do this."

Most said they teach a lot from Scripture, and since Jesus is the only way of salvation expressed in the New Testament, this message is communicated clearly and often with their youth. One youth pastor from California put it this way:

> This truth is dripped into every message, sermon, small group and devotional. You can't teach anything in a Christian ministry setting and not bring it back to the Bible and the fact that everything we believe hinges on the fact that Jesus lived, died, and lives again and He did this to give us relationship with Him and a purpose to life. Everything we teach must go back to this truth. If it does not it is only self-help and feel good advice and opinions. We can get that from a doctor, therapist, spiritualist or bar tender.

Another, from Wisconsin, put it this way:

> This is ingrained into everything we do. We teach this all the time because we teach the Bible and I don't see any way in which to teach the Bible without teaching that Jesus is the way, the truth, and the life and that no one comes to the Father except through Him.

The final three questions allowed the youth pastors to state specific examples of how they try to get this across to their students. Their response could be as long as they wished. They were also asked to identify the resources they use and whether they have experienced pushback from youth or parents in this regard.

Among the ideas that are not tied to a specific curriculum, one youth pastor from just outside of New York City divides his students into small groups every three years. Each group is assigned a topic related to pluralism or a specific religion other than Christianity. Each group can use a computer for research (their youth room has wifi); resource books are provided as well. On three successive weeks the students work in their groups to become "experts on their topic." In the next several weeks each group presents their material, which is then discussed in light of the historic Christian view.

Another youth pastor, this one from Michigan, likes to have some kind of mission or service trip every year. They may help with natural disaster cleanup in a different state or neighborhood cleanup in their own. They may go to a different country to partner with a church in their Vacation Bible School or in some other way. As a prerequisite to going on this trip, students must be able to articulate what they believe about Jesus and why they remain Christians instead of joining some other religion, designing their own faith à la carte or drop faith altogether. In preparation they role-play different scenarios and receive group feedback from their peers.

A youth pastor in Texas states he does not usually teach through particular books or chapters of the Bible, but rather he addresses topical themes such as identity or relationships. In his own words,

> When talking about identity I will highlight Jesus alone can give a real and life-giving identity. When talking about prayer I will highlight that because of Jesus alone we are able to approach God in prayer. When talking about relationship I will teach that Jesus alone offers the way to loving relationships.

If I were filling out the survey I would have highlighted an idea from my fourteen years as youth pastor in a Seattle church. Every fourth year I invited a different non-Christian professor from the

University of Washington to come to our senior high Sunday school class to explain why they had chosen not to be a Christian. This was not designed to be a debate, but students were allowed to ask questions for clarification. The idea was that two or three students would take careful notes during the presentation, and the following Sunday we reviewed and discussed the professor's talk point by point. My students found this a profoundly helpful experience.[19]

And as I expected, everyone wanted to be there. The place was jammed on these two Sundays, nearly a hundred students were present. Of the times we did this my favorite presenter was a female philosophy professor. Her lecture began with much bravado and confidence as she strode back and forth as if lecturing to hundreds in some grand Harvard auditorium. Our kids listened well, smiled respectfully and occasionally asked a question. About twenty minutes into her talk, she began to stumble verbally. Her ideas we not flowing, though her notes were in front of her. This got worse, and finally she just quit. She put down her notes, looked up at one hundred pairs of eyes looking at her and exclaimed, "God, I wish my thirteen-year-old daughter had a group like this to attend!"

Now that is quite a statement from an atheist! She thanked us for the opportunity and sat down. The applause our kids gave her was long and heartfelt. I thanked her for coming and ended the session. Immediately about twenty kids lined up to thank her personally, some gave her a hug and *asked about her daughter*. She was visibly shaken by this experience, as she had no categories for "Christian teenagers happy to be with each other, their leaders, the church and God."[20]

In the survey I asked about pushback. While most youth pastors did not identify anything specific, several did, most having to do with the cultural trend toward *tolerance*, which is taught at school. The following are some examples.

Our students are presented with so many differing views and options, it's hard for them to commit to a single way. (Nebraska)

I get questions that reflect that (it seems to me) our youth think Christianity is the best/only way in the same way they think their favorite sports team is the only one that deserves to win. So they are comfortable being on the "best team" but would probably struggle to come right out and say that all the other teams are going to hell. (Minnesota)

My students struggle with the "only way" because they fear if it gets out they believe this it will impact their reputation in a negative way. (Colorado)

Here push back in the context of small groups, when our kids get secure enough to be honest about their doubts. (Indiana)

My kids, even the ones from "good" Christian families, seem to have a grocery store mentality when it comes to religion . . . that anything can be added to their shopping cart. It makes me wonder if this stuff has ever been addressed at home by the parents. (Virginia)

Curious to get a feel from a Canadian point of view, I asked a friend from Vancouver about this. His response included, "a 'normal' culturally conditioned youth in Vancouver these days cannot even conceive of the idea that one faith is right and one wrong. When I say that one [faith] is right and the others wrong that is just viewed as part of 'my beliefs.'"

EXEMPLARY MINISTRIES

Among my own contacts in youth ministry are several who provide me with many examples of "best practices" in youth ministry in a multifaith society.

For eight years *Jerry* has been one of the youth pastors at a large Church of the Nazarene congregation in Virginia. He is an example of one who is proactively helping his youth navigate their way through a culture of tolerance and pluralism with their hearts, not just their heads. He says,

First of all, our student ministry clearly and loudly proclaims Jesus as the ONLY WAY to salvation, while maintaining a clear understanding that the trends of our society lean heavily toward that message not only being intolerant, but downright destructive. In a nutshell, the best way to kill a party is to start talking about the exclusivity of Jesus as the WAY to heaven.

In regards to training/discipleship, we challenge our students toward a "show, THEN tell" approach to sharing their faith. Where is my faith in Christ evidently seen (without being "showy")? How am I loving God by loving ALL people, regardless if they agree with me or not? And when we do have conversations that turn spiritual in nature, we must be sure to be "R.I.P." That is:

- **Respectful:** We aren't called to point out wrong as much as we're called to point to Jesus. I don't think Christians are called to argue souls into the Kingdom. We teach students that respect comes primarily from listening well, not speaking persuasively.

- **Intellectual:** We train our students to be intelligent about what they believe. We train our students that the teen years is prime time to let go of faith because your parents told you it's true (for example) and grab hold of faith because IT'S TRUE and we understand WHY it's true.

- **Personal:** Every person we interact with is a person Jesus died for. Non-Christians aren't projects and they aren't the enemy. They're the object of God's affection and it's up to us to convey that with light and salt.

He then goes on to explain the "True North" series he came up with about these issues. All emphasize the truth of the gospel (as traditionally understood but communicated in such as way as to emphasize that our role is to, as Jerry says, "show, then tell."

Dave is the lead youth pastor (of four) in a large evangelical church in New Jersey, where he has been for twelve years. Their student ministry has adopted the whole country of Ireland as a youth mission field and has planted two youth ministry centers that are now self-sustaining and have the enthusiastic blessing of local churches. Three additional youth ministry centers are under development and are close to being self-sustaining. Over lunch he recently told me that they have purchased, in the last six years, 275 round-trip tickets from Newark, New Jersey, to Dublin. By the time students in their ministry graduate from high school most have been to Ireland multiple times and engaged in various leadership roles on the field. And they sustain ongoing friendships with multiple Irish young people. It is quite apparent that most of the students who graduate out of this ministry do so with a traditional Christian faith that has been stretched and tested repeatedly.

Dave's ministry emphasizes that students know the Christian faith, but just as important to him is that they *feel* it and *experience* it as well. In this he is putting in action his understanding of the four learning styles; that is, most students learn best not by hearing or reading but by feeling and experiencing. In my opinion, outside of getting a graduate degree in education, the best description of the four learning styles is Marlene Lefever's *Learning Styles*.[21] Analytic learners (about 30% of youth and adults) love systematic information, enjoy taking notes, and look forward to teaching that involves sitting and listening. They also love predictability in a learning situation. Relational learners (25% of youth and adults) don't know what they are learning or what they think until they are talking about it with others; concepts emerge and gain clarity as they are processed with and through others verbally. Dynamic learners (about 28% of youth and adults) tune in when things are creatively done. They respond well to visual stimuli and they are happy to be surprised by what happens in a teaching-learning situation. And if they get to stand up, move around or do something with their hands during a teaching-learning situation, it makes them happy and motivated. Common sense learners (17% of youth and adults) may not say it out loud, but in their heads about every three minutes they are asking, *So what?* They embrace learning that is practical and immediately applicable to the situation at hand.

In all of the teaching that happens in Dave's youth ministry, the leaders are very aware that the vast majority of his students do not learn best via the sit-and-listen approach. He tries to hit all four learning styles in every teaching session that lasts more than twenty minutes.

Certainly the Irish mission is fraught with feelings and experiences, but the whole emphasis in their New Jersey youth ministry is to help youth know, feel and experience the faith.

This pedagogy comes together sublimely in their retreats. Here is Dave's description of one retreat.

We started off our retreat with a game as soon as the teens got there. We split into four different teams and students raced to find different pieces of a puzzle.

The puzzle pieces have parts of a clue that were written on with invisible ink and so to figure out the final clue they had to bring their puzzle pieces back to the main meeting room. There we had cut the meeting room in half with large dark curtains and had setup the back half of the room with black lights. All of this was to set up the main illustration of the night.

After the game was complete I gathered the group and had them write on their hands (privately) the different sins they all knew they needed to work on in their lives. We then read from Isaiah where Isaiah sees God and says, "Woe is me. For I am a man of unclean lips and I have seen the LORD Almighty." I asked them how they would feel if they went behind the curtain in the back half of the room again and I held up their hands to the black lights. I told them that standing before God that's exactly what it would be like . . . everything exposed. I then shared the truth about Jesus. How only his death had paid the price for their sins so that they could stand before God unashamed and be connected with Him.

We entered into a time of communion which we had set up behind them while I was speaking.

We set up large clear plastic cups in the shape of a cross (placed on a plastic sheet) and dipped the cups in red paint. We placed bread around the cross and surrounded it with candles.

As we sang a response song students were told to eat the bread and take the cup and wipe the red paint over their hands where they had written their sins to symbolize what Jesus had done for them and then enter behind the big curtain into God's presence. Behind the curtain we had started a blazing fire in a fireplace and so as they ate the bread and took the cup they covered their sins with the red paint that symbolized Jesus blood and walked into a completely dark room with nothing but an intense fire representing God's holiness and presence.

Kids stayed there on their face in complete silence for hours. It was reverent and silent and holy. One teen said to me after, "I couldn't get the blood off my hands!! I never realized it was my sin that He died for and it's my hands that put Him there." I said, "And it is your hands that He forgave and cleaned."

SUMMARY

In this chapter we have considered how youth workers try to reach out to nones and stem the flow of students who, knowingly or not, gravitate toward syncretism. I also made the point that awareness of basic adolescent cognitive development guides us in terms of what may be appropriate to present to teenagers at different stages of cognitive and moral development.

Next we will examine how to help our own students build bridges to sincere believers of other religions and deepen their own faith in the process.

CHRISTIAN ENGAGEMENT WITH OTHER RELIGIONS IN YOUTH WORK

Mission Possible 2

When I was a student at the University of Washington I took the required introduction to philosophy course. One day our professor asked, "If you are a born again Christian, please raise your hand." Of the two hundred or so students in the class, six (including me) raised their hands.

The professor then spent the next ten minutes berating us, telling the whole class we had no place in this class or the university, and expressing his hope that we would put away our childish, regressive religious ideas, grow up and enter the modern world. During his tirade against evangelical Christians I smiled faintly, my inner self was calm and I had one dominant thought: *I am so glad I've heard all this before. This poor guy doesn't know any better.*

You see, in high school I was part of debate club, and some of my closest friends there were atheists who reveled in their evangelistic zeal to deconstruct the Christian faith. I had another close friend who was a spiritist who enjoyed telling me about the "trumpet séances" he attended where, purportedly, a trumpet floated around the room talking. I also had the "problem" of two girls liking me *at the same time,* one of whom was a devout Mormon. By the time I was eighteen I had been forced to confront myriad hard questions about religion, faith and especially my historic Christian miracle-believing faith.

In an anthropology class the professor explained to us that all ancient cultures had a flood myth, and Christians were silly to believe that all the "mythology" in Genesis actually happened. I raised my hand: "But another way to look at it is that if all cultures around the globe have a flood myth, wouldn't that mean a worldwide flood actually happened?"

I concluded chapter one with a discussion of "positive doubt." This is the notion that as the adolescent brain gets its cognitive upgrade we should expose our students to other points of view regarding faith.[1] In this chapter we explore several ways to help young people have meaningful encounters with the "religious other" and subsequently have their own faith deepened.

BRIDGING TO OTHER FAITHS WITHOUT EVANGELISM BEING JOB ONE

In *Revisiting Relational Youth Ministry* Andrew Root provides a gentle but scathing rebuke to youth ministries and youth workers who seek to build relationship with teens for the sole purpose of winning them to Christ. He does not deny that evangelism is a legitimate concern, but he points out the hypocrisy of a youth worker building a relationship with a teen and then moving on if that teen is not responsive. It is hypocritical, says Root, in that Jesus loved people without regard to their acceptance of his message.[2]

Counterintuitively, a strong plea for Christians to develop a biblically based and theologically sound foundation for interfaith engagement and cooperation comes from Eboo Patel, a devout Muslim. He suggests such a biblical basis would include Jesus' story of the good Samaritan (Lk 10:25-37), his dealing with the Roman centurion (Lk 7:1-10) as well as his encounter with the Samaritan woman (Jn 4:5-42). Patel, founder and president of InterFaith Youth Core, says,

> Interfaith cooperation doesn't mean all religions are the same at the core, or our differences should be watered down. It also doesn't mean we don't have real disagreements and exclusive truth claims that may come into conflict with one another. It does mean, however, that we have shared values in common, values that diverse religious traditions insist their followers act on, like mercy, compassion, hospitality, and service.... As a Muslim, I am called to care for those who suffer in my community, called to be a good steward of creation, called to seek justice and mercy wherever I go. As a Christian, are you called to care about these things? And if so, can we work together on them?[3]

The needs of the poor and hurting of the world are so great, says Patel, that people of differing faiths who share common values should join together in their efforts to meet human needs. Here is the key for cooperation across religions. His organization, the InterFaith Youth Core, calls it "service learning." In this effort he tries to harness the common values found in all the world's religions: hospitality, co-operation, compassion and mercy.[4]

Joining with a Muslim youth group to clean up a community after a flood, for example, has at least four potential positives for our Christian youth. First, they will be connected with the heart of God in helping the hurting. Second, working alongside a Muslim may cause our students to think about their own faith. Christian students may ask questions of their faith they may not have been inclined to ask before. I want my students to ask questions and wonder about "the religious other" *now*, not in the future when they are away from home and in an environment that is potentially hostile to their faith.

Third, even though our service event may not have evangelism as the primary purpose, evangelism may indeed result from our efforts. Students from the other youth groups will see the resources the Christian faith offers. Fourth, I want to provide my students with opportunities to serve instead of being served. Growth in having a servant heart is a critical part of spiritual formation.

Even if our interfaith activities do not directly result in conversions (now or ever), if we have helped the hurting, we have connected to the heart of God for people. That in itself is good.

There is yet another way to look at student activity that helps the needy, whether alongside other religious young people or not. It comes from the missions perspective called the "Engle Scale" (see fig. 8.1). This simple conceptual scale posits that the road from no knowledge of God to becoming a fully functioning disciple of Christ involves incremental steps.[5] So, individuals and people groups we encounter are somewhere on the scale. Anything we do with others has the potential to move people up the scale. Though we may not see or experience the person come to faith in Christ, we were part of a chain of contacts leading to that point.

-8	No knowledge of God or the Christian religion
-7	Initial awareness of God or the Christian religion
-6	Awareness of the fundamentals of the gospel
-5	Grasp the implications of the gospel
-4	Positive attitude toward Christians and the gospel
-3	Recognition of personal need
-2	Decision to act
-1	Repentance and faith in Christ
+1	Post-decision evaluation
+2	Incorporation into body
+3	Conceptual and behavioral growth
+4	Communion with God
+5	Life stewardship in terms of the kingdom; able to disciple others

Figure 8.1. The Engle Scale

Some Christian thinkers observe that in the process of becoming a follower of Christ, a person tends to "belong before believing." That is, the interested person is first attracted to the believing community, and over time belonging to the community turns to belief. Then more of the content of the faith gets filled in as the person grows in Christ.[6] This does not negate the helpfulness of the Engle Scale; it affirms that the journey to becoming a Christian is often a multistep process. Our young people help others along that journey in any activity that reflects selfless giving and relational care.

Now that we have the conceptual basis for our student ministry proactively engaging with other faith communities, let's look at specific examples of how this is being done.

The Interfaith Youth Core is the most visible of the many organizations in the United States that promote interfaith activities, IFYC especially is geared for the college campus. Incorporated in 2002, their literature points out Martin Luther King Jr. and Mohandas Gandhi were both in the twenties when they began having an impact on society. The aspirations of IFYC are well expressed in the words

We view religious and philosophical traditions as bridges of cooperation. Our interfaith movement builds religious pluralism. We define religious pluralism as a world characterized by:

- Respect for people's diverse religious and non-religious identities.

- Mutually inspiring relationships between people of different backgrounds, and

- Common action for the common good.[7]

Their national office recommends a "leadership team" of students or faculty. Once gathered the team will plan and carry out events under the banner "Better Together." Among the many positives of

IFYC is the notion, expressed by their founder Eboo Patel, that interfaith activity does not mean participants give up the exclusive truth claims of their respective faiths but rather harness the compassion implicit in that faith for the good of others. Beyond the impulse for compassion found in many religions, Patel says interfaith work helps promote a civil society in a pluralistic cultural.[8]

To date there is no national organization that promotes interfaith activities at the high school level, but there are many local organizations doing just that. Examples include the Youth Interfaith Council in New Jersey, which sponsors multifaith social activities for the purpose of building relationships and having fun. It was founded by the youth workers of several area churches.[9] In the Twin Cities area the Interfaith Youth Leadership Coalition grew out of the St. Paul Area Council of Churches (SPACC.org). It focuses on collaborative projects that show compassion by helping the poor and hurting. The Muslim Jewish High School Leadership Council (muslimjew ishleadership.org) is a Los Angeles organization that does student leadership training (Muslim and Jewish youth being trained together) so those leaders can influence their own schools. The Puget Sound Interfaith Youth Camp (soundinterfaithcamp.org) provides an annual opportunity for students of different faiths to come together for a time of fun and mutual understanding. A new group for high school students in the Boston area has been started by the Interfaith Alliance (interfaithalliance.org).

YOUTH GROUP JOINT ACTIVITIES

Born in Birmingham, England, the "Feast" has a focus of bringing together Christian and Muslim youth and youth groups. Their three-step model can be used anywhere youth groups of different religions coexist. All it takes is at least one youth group leader from each faith to do the planning.

Step one is "exploring faith." In this gathering students eat together, play low-competition games and meet in small groups comprising equal number of Muslims and Christians. Around the circle, each student is given the opportunity to explain to the others what they like about their faith. This is not meant to be a debate but rather a sharing of personal feelings and information. After this round of sharing, students may ask questions of each other. Andrew Smith, founder of the Feast, observed when they began to do this most Christian young people were unable to fill their allotted five minutes; it appeared they had not given their faith any thought.[10] Subsequently he asked the leaders of Christian youth groups to help their own young people think about and discuss in advance what they like about their faith. This process helped in their own spiritual formation.

Step two is "creating friendships." Though this begins at the initial meeting, it really happens when the groups work on projects that help people in need. Smith observes that through mutual activity for the benefit of others come friendship, understanding and unity. He observes that *youths want friendship*.

Step three is "lives are changed." The friendships continue beyond the service projects and the positive feelings about people of different faith transfer to families, siblings and other friends. More projects and events are eventually planned and led by the students themselves, which has a significant positive impact on their own lives.

The ministry approach and purpose of the Feast has been endorsed in the United Kingdom by both Christian church leaders and leaders within the Muslim community who have agreed on "Ethical Guidelines for Christian and Muslim Witness in Britain."

The Christian Muslim Forum offers the following suggestions that will equip Christians and Muslims (and others) to share their faith with integrity and compassion for those they meet.

1) We bear witness to, and proclaim our faith not only through words but through our attitudes, actions and lifestyles.

2) We cannot convert people, only God can do that. In our language and methods we should recognize that people's choice of faith is primarily a matter between themselves and God.

3) Sharing our faith should never be coercive; this is especially important when working with children, young people and vulnerable adults. Everyone should have the choice to accept or reject the message we proclaim and we will accept people's choices without resentment.

4) Whilst we might care for people in need or who are facing personal crises, we should never manipulate these situations in order to gain a convert.

5) An invitation to convert should never be linked with financial, material or other inducements. It should be a decision of the heart and mind alone.

6) We will speak of our faith without demeaning or ridiculing the faiths of others.

7) We will speak clearly and honestly about our faith, even when that is uncomfortable or controversial.

8) We will be honest about our motivations for activities and we will inform people when events will include the sharing of faith.

9) Whilst recognizing that either community will naturally rejoice with and support those who have chosen to join them, we will be sensitive to the loss that others may feel.

10) Whilst we may feel hurt when someone we know and love

chooses to leave our faith, we will respect their decision and will not force them to stay or harass them afterwards.[11]

Certainly one does not need to be part of the Feast franchise to have youth groups of different faiths come together for understanding. It is helpful, however, to benefit from the wisdom garnered by others who have chosen to go down this road. For example, Andrew Smith has observed that many of the Muslim young people he knows are children of immigrants. They do not have freedom, within the context of their own families, to choose their religion. He feels it's unethical to encourage a teenager to convert to another religion and then tell the teen to keep it a secret from his or her family. Smith believes that many of these young people will step toward Christianity when they are university age and on their own. The point here is to be sensitive to the home environment of the young person.

CHURCH-BASED AFTERSCHOOL PROGRAMS

No national organization tracks the number of church-based afterschool programs for children and youth. School-based programs increased beginning in 2002 when the Clinton administration committed a billion dollars to these programs in rural and urban communities, spawning programs in 7,500 schools.[12]

In communities where these programs have been defunded or where the number of programs fall short of the need, churches try to meet the needs of their communities through their own afterschool programs. The parents of many teenagers, for example, are not home when school dismisses, and the schools themselves have no afterschool programs of any kind. In this situation a church can make available their facilities for recreation, arts or homework. Depending on the community makeup, these young people may be of another religion or none at all.

Churches seeking to meet real community needs through an afterschool program do not have to reinvent the wheel to do so. A good source of collected wisdom is *Saving Souls, Serving Society: Understanding the Faith Factor in Church-Based Social Ministry*, which provides a case study approach to different scenarios.[13] A comprehensive step-by-step guide for starting such programs, applicable to schools and churches, has been produced by the state of Utah.[14] It covers licensing, organizational structure, risk management recruiting and hiring, and training.

The Salvation Army has combined with Scripture Union to similarly provide guidelines and programming for afterschool programs specifically for churches. Called "PrimeTime," its focus is young people ages six through twelve. The program includes startup guidelines, curricular resources and staff training resources.[15]

All of the approaches discussed in this chapter have great potential to foster the spiritual formation of our own students and help them make the Christian faith their own faith. They are also likely to help others move a step closer to commitment to Christ. Now let's look at how Jesus engaged those who were not yet partakers of the kingdom of God.

JESUS AND THE KINGDOM OF GOD: FOUR ENCOUNTERS

During his three-year ministry on earth, Jesus had four different types of encounters with others: the love encounter, the truth encounter, the power encounter, and the allegiance encounter.

Love encounter. Jesus repeatedly demonstrated love that was surprising and unconventional. For example, he initiated an extended conversation with a Samaritan woman (Jn 4). Not only was she a *woman*, she was a *religious outsider*. So the reader won't miss the significance, the author of the Fourth Gospel says, "For Jews do not associate with Samaritans" (Jn 4:9).

When Jesus' dear friend Lazarus died (Jn 11), Jesus not only wept in grief but did something astonishing to express love: *he raised Lazarus from the dead!* It is interesting to note that while Jesus called to Lazarus ("Lazarus, come out!" [v. 43]) he involved the community in releasing Lazarus from his grave clothes (v. 44). Now there is a community-building exercise!

Jesus cared for and loved his disciples until they "got it." He certainly gave them his time. The further along he went in ministry, the more time he spent with them. He articulated his love and called them "friends" (Jn 15:9-17). With at least one disciple who was slow to understand (Peter), he had a personal counseling session (Jn 21:15-19).

Jesus was indeed God's love incarnate.

When I first came to a church to serve as youth pastor, the students were *brutal* to each other. The group was rife with gossip, arguments flared up often, and the f-bomb was hurled at others. This dysfunction was one of the group's attractions to me. I knew I would have to be dependent on and in tune with the power of God to foster change in the group. I arrived on the scene in the spring and observed the sorry spiritual state of many of the student leadership team. When June came I instituted a new selection procedure for the leadership team. I gave the students a list of all the group members and asked them to circle the names of up to five males and five females who, in their opinion, were most committed to the group *and* to Christ.

I then began to meet regularly with these students. In our opening meeting I asked them to share why they were willing to commit to leadership. (Many were in despair over the disunity and meanness in the group.) I asked them to come up with a list of mutual commitments for being in leadership. As they talked, I guided them toward four areas: commitment (1) to God, (2) to each other, (3) to all members of the youth group, and (4) to myself and the adult staff.

Our bimonthly leadership meeting typically included the following: (1) We prayed for each other and discussed our accountability regarding our own walk with God.[16] (2) We each answered the accountability question: Who in the group did I speak with in the last two weeks that I normally do not speak with? (3) We evaluated the previous two weeks of youth group gatherings, such as our weekly youth group night, Sunday school, and (for example) basketball and pizza night. (4) We planned for upcoming events. (5) We had a brief training time (e.g., What does it mean to *listen* to someone?) (6) We got on our knees and prayed for the youth group members and our plans.

Over time, the *emotional climate* of the group shifted dramatically toward the positive. In my mind God used two things to cause this change. Now we had at least ten students who committed to speaking to someone outside their friendship clusters. These leadership students weren't asked to abandon their clique but to speak *once* with someone outside their norm. This had a ripple effect. Often a student leader would bring a close friend to speak to this "other." Second, the time spent on our knees changed the mindset of the student leaders from *consumer* to *provider*.

I also used this approach in a large youth group representing twenty-six high schools, and the result was the same! The group became welcoming, friendly, open and, eventually, loving. (In both situations we also instituted small groups as part of the normal youth group menu.)

How does this fit in with Jesus' love encounters? When a new person invited by a friend came to our youth group meetings, they would experience love and acceptance. After coming a couple of times, it wasn't unusual for that person to ask the equivalent of "What must I do to be saved?" What they saw in these peers, they wanted for themselves.

Many students of Muslim background will find the emotional climate of a church youth group a dramatic change from what they are accustomed to. As we saw in chapter two, only 18 percent of mosques in the United States have a youth program, and the percentage is not much higher in most other countries. If they attend the mosque at all, they experience (endure?) preaching and teaching aimed entirely at adults. Often, young people are neither acknowledged nor valued by adults other than their parents.[17] In a church youth group they find the opposite. They are cared about as individuals, and their needs, interests and problems are addressed from a biblical point of view.

Truth encounter. The word *truth* is used twenty times in the Gospel of John alone, including the famous words of Jesus "You will know the truth, and the truth shall set you free" (Jn 8:32) and "I am the way and the truth and the life. No one comes to the Father except through me" (Jn 14:6). Clearly Jesus spoke and taught the truth. Indeed, he is the truth! When the truth of Christ is taught, students of all persuasions experience a cognitive and behavioral paradigm shift.

Virtually all student ministries stemming from the traditional Christian perspective emphasize teaching the truth. All of the Evangelical Free Church youth pastors who responded to my survey (see chap. 5) indicated that *teaching* is a huge piece of their ministries.

An important question, however, is what constitutes effective teaching? Jesus' parables, illustrations and stories used items from everyday life. At the very least teaching in youth ministry needs to follow this pattern. I try to facilitate a teaching model that is filled with Scripture illustrated by examples, stories and references to everyday reality. As I mentioned earlier in the book, I encourage student involvement when I teach. I speak for only a fraction of the time allotted.[18] While a typical youth lesson I lead is thirty minutes, much of the interaction is in pairs or small groups.

Our student ministries might include newcomers who are hungry for truth. They may be experiencing emptiness stemming from narcissism or a postmodernism worldview. Or a student from another religious background may wonder what a Christian friend has that serves as an internal gyroscope, keeping her friend steady and on course despite the storms of normal adolescent life. Or a Hindu student might be interested in the simple truth of the gospel. Compared to the many gods of Hinduism and the pressure to live right without anything other than self-effort, the gospel is indeed good news.

Power encounter. Any miracle, be it healing or otherwise, is a kind of power encounter that is not of this world. When missiologists speak of power encounters, however, they are often referring to the demonic. Jesus routinely cast out demons as part of his own ministry (e.g., Mk 1:34, 39). He expected his disciples to do this as well (Mk 3:14-15). The disciples' success in power encounters was lumpy. For example, after an especially embarrassing failure Jesus said they had "little faith" (Mt 17:14-20).

Unless we are part of a Pentecostal or charismatic church, power encounters are unlikely to be a routine part of student ministry. I help my own students understand the power encounters are real in several ways. I don't ignore power encounter texts in Scripture. I invite missionaries to explain how they experience power in their own ministries. I emphasize "The one who is in you is greater than the one who is in the world" (1 Jn 4:4) and that we have nothing to fear when it comes to the demonic. Furthermore, I explain that should they realize they are in a demonic situation, as believers they can trump any satanic presence or influence following the pattern of Paul in Acts 16:18: "In the name of Jesus Christ I command you to come out!"

I've had to do this once in front of the whole youth group. That was a teachable moment! We had about thirty students helping to present the evening service at the local Union Gospel Mission. In this facility, homeless and hungry men sat through a service and then got a hot meal and a place to sleep. Our students led worship and gave their testimonies. I preached. During my sermon I moved from the platform to be closer to the audience, and a man sitting ten feet from me rose to his feet and threw a hymnal at me. It hit my shoulder and continued its trajectory to a nearby wall—bang!

I walked right over to him, and pointing my finger at his heart I said, "In the name of Jesus I command you to come out of him!"[19] The guy immediately fell backward over his chair onto the floor, and as the security people were running forward from the back of the auditorium, the man was exclaiming, "That man threw the devil out of me!" When the security people got to the man, I told them they were no longer needed. After the man righted his chair and sat calmly, I continued my sermon. *You can well imagine that in the church bus on the way home I had thirty students who were eager to unpack what happened.*

We don't have to be an exorcist, however, to help students understand this. In addition to what has already been suggested, mission trips are a good way to help students experience spiritual warfare. I ask them if they felt "darkness" at any point during the day. In this I'm trying to help them understand there is an unseen world and some of that unseen world is malevolent.

In the Gospels power encounters had evangelistic impact. There is no reason the same cannot be true in youth ministry today.[20]

The county in which I live is 35 percent Jewish, and this population is divided into two very different groups. The Orthodox-Hassidic group is insular and are not open to those outside their group. The other group of Jews is the opposite. They are liberal in theology, attend synagogue only rarely and are essentially secular in perspective. For many young people of this background the Jewish religion is not relevant. For these young people the notion that God is alive and actually does stuff in the lives of their Christian peers is both interesting and astonishing. It doesn't take an exorcism or dramatic healing to gain their attention. They may sense God's reality in a youth group worship experience or listen with drop-jawed amazement as a peer testifies how she had a dramatic answer to prayer or an undeniable sense of God's personal direction.

Allegiance encounter. An allegiance encounter is a volitional challenge. Jesus often called people to align themselves with him and his kingdom. The early chapters of the Synoptic Gospels include the calling of the disciples. Among the many interactions with others we see that not everyone said yes to his invitation. When Jesus encountered a rich young man, telling him to sell all he had and give it to the poor before following Jesus, the text says, "At this the man's face fell. He went away sad, because he had great wealth" (Mk 10:22).

Student ministries with the traditional biblical understanding see "reaching students for Christ" as an essential component of ministry. An immense amount of programming creativity is poured into outreach events.

I'm attracted to a pattern in which there are two kinds of outreach events. The first is for the sake of fun and building community. At these we have no prayer and no devotional. There is nothing overtly spiritual. Guests are invited (and they do come!) and they have a great time. As a byproduct they discover that Christians have fun without getting drunk or high. Second, every three months or so we have an event where we gather as part of the evening and the gospel is explained (usually by a student), and an opportunity is provided for some kind of response.

My favorite of these is what I call a student-led "in-house" outreach event. About once every five or six weeks, instead of a normal youth group meeting, we have this special night. It is completely student led; no adults are up front. The night has a theme (e.g., friendship). The program is in four sections. Games/fun stuff, which has something to do (however loosely) with friendship, comes first. Then we have media or skits that support the theme. Next, three students explain how Jesus has made a difference in their lives when it comes to friendship. Finally, the last student to give the friendship talk concludes with something like "If this interests you and you want to find out how you can come to know Christ like a friend and have him make a huge difference in your life, when we do "name grabbers" next, just put a big X on the back of your name grabber and we'll find you during the ice cream sundae time so we can talk."

Name grabbers are 3 x 5 cards that ask for the students' name and contact information. We do this in youth group every week, and there is a drawing at the end for some kind of prize. We collect the name grabbers and dismiss people to the food area. At that point three student leaders quickly go through the pile of cards looking for "X." When found, it is determined who will speak with whom. (Only students speak with the "X" students, not adults.) It's not unusual to have students cross that line to living faith as a result of these outreach nights. Students from other faith traditions, especially those traditions and cultures that are adult centered, are quite shocked to see peers providing religious leadership.

A MULTIFAITH PASTORAL THEOLOGY

Presence and Power in Youth Work

I love to design and carry out ministry programs that are explicitly outreach oriented. That is, I'm looking for on-ramps to the Christian faith that students of no faith, syncretistic faith or other faiths can travel. I've made many mistakes in the process. Some of these mistakes are funny now; some of them will never be. Here are two examples.

I'm probably the only youth worker in all of history to hold a youth retreat in a house of prostitution.

Thinking back, the sign behind the registration desk did strike me as odd: "No illegal activities allowed on the premises." Having confirmed that the motel had received our full payment in the mail a month earlier, I walked back out to help the senior highers unload the church bus. The retreat was going great. We had slept on the floor of a church near Whistler Mountain, British Columbia, on Friday night, skied all day Saturday, and were excited about the rest of the weekend in the beautiful city of Vancouver. City Motel was now our headquarters.

A police car roared in from Main Street and stopped a yard from me. The officer got out and approached. Looking confused or lost or something, he asked, "What are you doing?"

"Well, officer," I replied, "As you see here, we're unloading the church bus. We're from Seattle; we were at Whistler today, and now we're going to stay here."

"Don't you know what this is?"

My life began to pass in front of me. "What do you mean?"

"This is a house of prostitution, serves this end of the city. Better keep a close watch on your kids."

"Thanks . . ." My voice trailed off as he returned to his patrol car.

My mind was a blur. We had no money, there was no place else to stay, and most of the kids heard this conversation. No wonder City Motel was so cheap; just wait till news of this one gets out: "Youth Pastor Jailed for His Own Protection as Angry Parents Picket Church."

Fortunately, our bus driver was a respected church elder. I called him aside. With a gleam in his eye he said, "I think God wants us to overtake this place." That's all I needed to hear, because I was starting to think the same thing.

We moved into our rooms. They were so dirty most of us went right back to the bus to get our sleeping bags. The hotel towels were paper thin and stained. I crammed everyone into my room and we discussed our situation. Then followed a wonderful (and loud) time of worship and prayer right there.

Just as the officer predicted, it was a very busy night. Male and female customers came and went all night. Most of us didn't sleep very well. We were glad to get out the door and on to Grouse Mountain for more skiing the next day. When we got home, the elder took the initiative to call key parents and explain what happened.

My students, Christian or not, saw and experienced a sense of God's presence in the hotel room worship service.

Here is a second story. Wasn't funny then, still isn't.

Dear Pastor Kageler,

With regards to your so-called youth rally next month, I am writing to inform you again that I feel what you have planned is a godless abomination. I am writing our denominational headquarter and our Christian college presidents, as well as the other pastors in our district to ask them to join me in fasting and prayer, and to call upon God to stop this evil. You will be held accountable by Almighty God for the worldliness you are fostering among our precious young people.

I intend to do everything in my power to stop this event.[1]

Again, as was the case with the ski retreat at Whistler, this youth rally's (a lip-sync contest) purpose was to interest and engage not only Christian students but others as well. I've learned to expect problems, and my observation is that any youth worker who seeks to guide students toward the Christian faith will encounter difficulties. It's all the more important then to get our theology, particularly our Christology, right.

BUILDING ON A GOOD FOUNDATION

In the last twenty years there have been several attempts to help youth workers see Christian youth ministry within a theological framework. These authors are offering, each in their own way, a cognitive gyroscope for ministry. Here we will acknowledge the positive contributions of these theological approaches. I want to then make a new contribution.

Used by youth ministry professors for many years as a required text for youth ministry education, Richard Dunn and Mark Senter's *Reaching a Generation for Christ* speaks of systematic theology in terms of "building blocks" for ministry.[2] Several of the major topics of systematics (God, Scripture, humanity, sin, salvation and the church) are not only explained but both personal and student-ministry implications are explored. Dunn and Senter see youth workers as "theological construction workers."[3]

A few years later another heavy text entered the field. *Starting Right: Thinking Theologically About Youth Ministry* takes an opposite approach to theology and praxis. Whereas Dunn and Senter started with theology and later moved to ministry implications, *Starting Right* begins with specific aspects of ministry and posits how each aspect can be understood theologically.[4] Topics such as ministry models, evangelism, family, student leadership, community and innovation are addressed. Much more recently Andrew Root and Kenda Creasy Dean considered theological connections with a variety of programmatic components and emotional states common in student ministry.[5]

Five years later two books entered the field from a theological and spiritual formation point of view, focusing particularly on the personal spirituality of the youth worker. For example, *Presence-Centered Youth Ministry* envisions the youth worker as functioning out of the overflow of God's presence in her or his own life.[6] *Contemplative Youth Ministry* provides fresh vocabulary for this interior spiritual life and focuses on what it means to practice the presence of Jesus.[7]

Shortly thereafter *Jesus-Centered Ministry* emphasized Jesus as the proper center of *all* youth ministry. Rick Lawrence, taking his cue from the nineteenth-century sermons of C. H. Spurgeon, brings the reader back to the point that made Spurgeon's ministry so comprehensively powerful: all aspects of ministry have their basis in the person and work of Jesus Christ.[8]

THE LIVING CHRIST AND HOW WE SEE OURSELVES AND MINISTRY

My own heart is very much in the same stream as Rick's *Jesus-Centered Ministry*, but I wish to consider more specifically the challenges of multifaith-society youth ministry. I began this book with a declaration that our Christology uniquely connects us with both Jesus' *presence* and *power* as we engage in student ministry in a multifaith society. In this chapter we'll explore Christology expressed in (1) the seven "I am" statements of Jesus in the Gospel of John, (2) the two most important paired words in the entire New Testament, "In Christ," and (3) how Jesus as Suffering Servant can connect the dots in praxis. These aspects of Christology can equip us to be persons of presence and power, and help our students navigate their multifaith world.

Jesus' "I am" statements. How did Jesus understand himself? It's not possible for us to grasp what it would have been like to be "very God and very man."[9] In the Gospel of John we especially see Jesus trying to interpret himself, often in metaphor. There were almost always three different audiences present when Jesus said "I AM." His disciples, already believers, were there. The second group is those who gathered around Jesus for a variety of reasons. They may have seen a healing or heard of one. They knew that Jesus was *somehow different.* The religious leaders comprised the third group. They were generally skeptical, cynical or hostile.

So then, this in a very real way parallels our own audiences in Christian youth ministry. Some of our students believe (group 1). We know (and try to reach) students who are or may be open to Jesus (group 2). We may also know students or parents who are skeptical, cynical or hostile, whether they are committed to a different faith or to no faith at all (group 3).

The bread of life. Having just fed the five thousand it was getting dark and Jesus tried to slip away to get some downtime on the other side of the lake. Crossing the lake by boat was a tad traumatic for the disciples, but they made it. Perhaps Peter tweeted about it or posted it on his Facebook page, because the next morning the crowds arrived. To them Jesus eventually said, "I am the bread of life. Whoever comes to me will never go hungry, and whoever believes in me will never be thirsty" (Jn 6:35).

Jesus was saying there is something more important than physical food and drink. A relationship with him sustains us in a very different way. Seeing Jesus as the bread of life gives us the possibility of life with unlimited reserves. It makes it possible for us to be able to recover from ministry setbacks. It prevents us from losing hope or becoming cynical when a youth group member makes a poor choice.

Many of our students who are of no faith or of another faith have already realized their own "bread" is not satisfying for the long term. They will see the difference and be drawn to have this bread.

The light. We can't be sure from the text if Jesus' "I am the light" statement immediately follows his confrontation with the Pharisees over the woman caught in adultery (Jn 8:1-11). It probably did because the Pharisees, now angry that he made them look bad in front of the people, were instantly hostile when Jesus then says "I am the light of the world. Whoever follows me will never walk in darkness, but will have the light of life" (Jn 8:12).

To the crowds that heard this sharp interaction between the Pharisees, Jesus was a fresh voice with a point of view they'd never heard. The religious leaders lived and taught "follow the law or else." Jesus, by contrast, said, "Follow me. I'll be your way to see forward."

Jesus as light invites us into a life of clarity and direction. To our students it is an invitation to connect their stories to a much larger story, and to discover what it means to no longer walk in darkness. I have seen students of no faith and other faiths tune in when a peer tells their story (we used to call this a testimony). In the current youth group I serve, the nones and students from other religions are most apt to ask follow-up questions or seek one-on-one discussion with a peer leader or adult leader when a peer narrates his or her own life walk with Jesus.

The gate. Jesus contrasted himself to the false or useless gates the religious leaders were teaching about.[10] "I am the gate; whoever enters through me will be saved. They will come in and go out, and find pasture. The thief comes only to steal and kill and destroy. I have come that they may have life, and have it to the full" (Jn 10:9-10). Those who heard this must have been dumbfounded to hear someone heap scorn on the religious leaders.

Seeing Jesus as a doorway or gate to a life beyond the self opens us up to feelings of worth and deep happiness.[11] And who of our students or their parents do not want life "to the full"?

In student ministry I have often hosted what amounts to community outreach events aimed at parents of teenagers. Of course it is not marketed as such. Generally I have rented a room at the local middle school as the venue. My favorite seminar title is "Thriving, Not Just Surviving the Strong-Willed Teenager." My observation is that parents of teenagers whose behavior is wreaking havoc are desperate for help. I've seen parents with no faith, syncretistic faith or another faith come hungry for help. My approach is to have at least ten Christian parents attend who have seen Christ make a difference in their homes. It's fascinating to watch the intense interest (by nones, for example) when this new (to them) narrative is put on the table.

The good shepherd. The next "I am" statement is part of the same conversation about the gate and sheep. "I am the good shepherd. The good shepherd lays down his life for the sheep" (Jn 10:11). Now Jesus' hearers are given an even starker picture of the contrast between the religious leaders and himself. The religious leaders are like thieves and robbers, only "shepherds" for the income generated. Jesus cares enough for sheep that he'd sacrifice his life if one were in danger.

This is one of my favorite "I am" statements. I find it comforting to think of my life being shepherded well. It is an affirmation of Jesus' caring for us just as the Father does in Psalm 23: "The Lord is my shepherd, I shall not be in want . . ."

Our students notice when we convey a sense of personal flourishing and at the same time have a caring (shepherding) heart toward them. Struggling parents too may deeply appreciate our efforts on behalf of their own children. I long ago lost count of the expressions of gratitude from these parents for care their sons and daughters have experienced in the youth group. With tears in their eyes, secular, angry, single mothers, for example, have expressed thanks for the good influence a Christian youth group has on their teens. I also have had immigrant parents of Hindu background express relief that their daughter is identifying with a Christian youth group.

Resurrection and the life. John 11 tells the story of Lazarus's death and resurrection. Jesus purposely arrived after Lazarus had died. He was so late, in fact, that his friend was already buried (v. 17). Lazarus's sisters, Mary and Martha, were grieving, struggling with thoughts of "what if" and "if only" Jesus had come while Lazarus was still living. Jesus told Martha, who had come out of the house to meet him, "Your brother will rise again" (v. 22). Martha, perhaps in a forlorn tone, sighs, "I know he will rise again in the resurrection at the last day" (v. 24). And then she hears him say, "I am the resurrection and the life. The one who believes in me will live, even though they die" (vv. 25-26). This takes on deeper meaning when the grave stone is pushed aside and Jesus commands, "Lazarus, come out" (v. 43). I wish we had a YouTube clip of Lazarus shuffling out of the grave, bound in grave wrappings. Perhaps we would hear a very muffled voice saying, "Help me out here, please!"

Here we see that Jesus is in the restoration business. He does extreme makeovers. We may think we have made a mistake that is unforgivable and our life is ruined. Not so. This is a wonderful Scripture to bring to students or parents who are suffering the results of a setback or life-altering catastrophe. We know that personal catastrophe is no respecter of age, sex or religion, and we offer hope and help to those whose need is acute.

The way, the truth, and the life. The disciples were disoriented and upset that their three-year road trip with Jesus was soon to end. Thomas blurts out his confusion, "Lord, we don't know where you are going!" and Jesus answers, "I am the way and the truth and the life. No one comes to the Father except through me" (Jn 14:5-6). The disciples struggled to get their heads around what was happening, and as the conversation unfolds some of them show glimmers of comprehension. (It all became much clearer in the presence of a resurrected Christ a few days later.)

I see the first part of verse 6 as an invitation to a life of *purpose.* As we respond to Jesus' loving initiative, he becomes the center of our lives. And of course the second half of the verse, "No one comes to the Father except through me," is among the key verses for those of us who espouse the traditional Christian faith. This verse is also a key to the church's entire missionary enterprise. We understand there is only *one* way. This impels us to make our student ministry welcoming to those who are not yet believers. My friends who hold afterschool programs in neighborhoods that are predominantly Muslim or Hindu tell me that these parents and their kids see something different in them. They want to learn more of this Jesus.

The vine. In John 15 we are invited into a holy huddle of Jesus and the disciples. Here Jesus uses the analogy of connectivity. "I am the true vine, and my Father is the gardener. . . . I am the vine; you are the branches. If you remain in me and I in you, you will bear much fruit; apart from me you can do nothing" (Jn 15:1, 5). All his hearers knew the vine-branch image and what happens when a branch is cut off. And in verse 15 Jesus says their relationship is even more personal, and he calls them "friends."

This connectivity is for us as well. When things go bad in our lives, our connection to Christ and his followers is the key to flourishing. When things go bad in our ministries, these connections count as well. In the opening stories of this chapter, for example, it was the sense of Jesus' presence, the sense of his friendship, that sustained me.

Connection with Jesus makes possible deep and authentic connection with others. That sense of connection, love and fellowship can be sensed by a newcomer to our youth group. It is one of the most powerful apologetics we have for a vital faith in Christ. We offer *presence*.[12]

Recently, I was working with several youth group members at our church's booth at the Nyack Street Fair. We handed out 1,100 bottles of cold water to some very grateful passersby. We were having a great time with each other as we served others, and we received several comments about this from those we served. There was obviously some deep connection we had. Even in receiving water and a smile, people saw *presence* that day.

"In Christ." Whereas the "I am" statements help us realize and experience Jesus' *presence*, "in Christ," used by Paul seventy-three times, helps us realize and experience Jesus' *power*. Paul's belief that being "in Christ" is the central descriptor of the Christian and the source of daily living power. Paul states that if we are in Christ it means that the same Spirit who raised Jesus from the dead resides in us as well (Rom 8:10-11). This chapter of Romans contrasts two kinds of lives. One is life outside Christ, the other life in him.

The old way of life, the life outside Christ, can be summarized in my paraphrase of Joshua 1:8, "Here is the law, just do it." The problem is, of course, no one is able to do it, at least not for long. In 2 Corinthians Paul describes it as a letter that kills (v. 6). By contrast "in Christ," where the power to please God does not stem from our own discipline and effort but rather Christ's power in us, is described by Paul as a letter of life (v. 6). He states plainly that because of this new covenant (this new way of living in Christ) we have confidence "through Christ before God." Not that we are competent to claim anything for ourselves, but our competence comes from God" (2 Cor 3:4-5).

I did not fully appreciate the concepts of the "new covenant" and being "in Christ" until I read *The Normal Christian Life*. Watchman Nee explained the new covenant in shocking language:

> What does it mean in everyday life to be delivered from the Law? At risk of a little overstatement I reply: It means that henceforth I am going to do nothing whatever for God; I am never again going to try to please Him. "What a doctrine!" you exclaim. "What awful heresy! You cannot possibly mean that!" But remember, if I try to please God "in the flesh," then immediately I place myself under the Law.[13]

Nee explains that God, in Christ, is much more interested in living through us than having us try hard and then helping us out when we come up short.

Incensed by this preposterous claim, I pulled out a Bible concordance and looked up all the Old Testament verses that contained the word *help* as part of a prayer or affirmation of what God does. There are over forty such instances. I went to the New Testament with the same question. How many times in the New Testament is the word *help* used in prayer? Zero! In the Gospels various people asked Jesus to help them (e.g., Mt 15:25), but there are no such prayers in the Epistles.

This radically altered my prayer life and my view of what it means to be a Christian. I no longer ask God for help with anything. In the morning instead of praying "Lord, help me to live like you want today" I say, "Lord, I'm all yours. I'll step aside and enjoy your wonderful self as you operate through me today." Jon Acuff says something similar: "God has no interest in better. He is, on the other hand, all about new."[14]

This made a big difference in how I felt about the Christian life. Previously, if someone asked, "Would you say living as a Christian life is hard or easy?" I would, without hesitation, answer "It's quite hard, but basically doable much of the time." Now my answer is "Quite easy actually."[15]

This perspective is immensely helpful when facing the challenges and crises of everyday life, including those of student ministry. Living "in Christ" gives us power to get up each day and function in a kingdom-connected way. Our students too can experience this.

This can help us with our interactions with youth and parents of other faiths. The adherents of Islam, Hinduism, Buddhism and all other religions strive to fulfill what is expected of them. For example, Muslim youth work places a high priority on teaching students to work hard to stay on the correct path.[16] By contrast, being "in Christ" releases the person from self-effort. This perspective is filled with grace and empowerment. This is exactly what Muslim high school students notice (or should notice) when they show up at Christian youth group gatherings.

Being "in Christ," however, does not exempt us from sorrow and pain.

The Suffering Servant. Isaiah 52–53 introduces the notion that the Messiah will be a servant who suffers. How does our belief in the Suffering Servant inform our lives as believers and our efforts to facilitate student ministry in a society full of other faiths or no faith at all?[17]

Jesus suffered in at least four respects. He suffered *physically*, of course. The desert experience described in Luke 1 was not held at an upscale retreat center with a breakfast buffet. We see in the Gospels that Jesus was sometimes exhausted and needed to get away from the pressing crowds. And the cross? Enough said.

Jesus suffered *spiritually*. Before the crucifixion he pleaded with his Father to exempt him from what was to happen (Lk 22:42-44). And on the cross he felt the cold terror of abandonment by God (Mk 15:34).

Jesus have suffered *intellectually*. Despite his repeated explanations of his nature and mission to his disciples and the crowds, most just did not get it. Imagine his chagrin when he heard his disciples arguing over which of them would be the greatest (Mt 18:1).

We know Jesus suffered *emotionally* as he saw physical, mental and spiritual pain of people (Lk 19:41). He felt the loss when his friend Lazarus died (Jn 11:35).

And we suffer as well in student ministry. We are physically tired after a lock-in or retreat. We are sad when ten kids show up to an event when we expected fifty. We are grieved when our brightest and best students make poor choices and are unrepentant. We lie awake at night over an unkind comment by a student. We suffer spiritually when we cry out to God for this key student, that big program or that well-meaning but angry parent who has turned against us. We also suffer spiritually when we are so tired we fall asleep while praying or reading the Bible.

And we all experience, over time, the healing, comfort, solace and restoration that comes from the presence of the living Christ and the dear people around us who re-present him to us when we can't see him for ourselves.

But sometimes suffering enables us to make kingdom progress in our efforts to see lost people come to faith. This happens in two respects.

Our own suffering may be a powerful apologetic to the students and parents of other faiths or no faith. When our suffering is public, people are watching. If they see something in us that, despite our suffering, gives us the ability to put one foot in front of the other each day and still thank God and care about others, it is a powerful witness. It may cause others to seriously examine their own life foundations and question whether they would have the same resources in a similar situation.

This is very much in the same vein as the evangelistic impact of ancient Romans watching Christians getting mauled by lions or roasted in the flames at the local arena. For some it was great sport. For others, watching this cruelty deconstructed their Roman life assumptions, causing them to wonder, *What do Christians have that I don't?*[18]

This is not the only way in which suffering may trigger spiritual interest by others.

When a student or parent experiences tragedy, we may find them open as never before to the gospel. I have a good friend who is the head chaplain of a large pediatric hospital in the United Kingdom. The hospital has a staff of ten chaplains; religions other than Christianity are well represented on his staff. Almost every day he sees how having a child in severe health crisis is the great leveler of race, class, gender and religion. One aspect of this that initially puzzled him, but which he now accepts as normal, is that about half of the adherents of other religions desperately want *Christians* to pray for their child. And if death comes, even a higher percentage want an explicitly Christian funeral.

Keith Miller said, we Christians "lightly run our fingers over a person's soul until we find a crack, and then gently pour our love into that crack."[19] A crisis opens a crack, a chasm really. People know they need something they do not themselves possess. C. S. Lewis observed, "Pain insists upon being attended to. God whispers to us in our pleasures, speaks in our consciences, but shouts in our pains. It is his megaphone to rouse a deaf world."[20]

In youth work we are strategically placed to help hurting persons experience a living Christ in the midst of their own suffering and sorrow. We may even be able to introduce them to a Savior who was a man of sorrows, acquainted with grief (Is 53:3 ESV), and his Father, who lost a Son.

CONCLUSION

The first two chapters began with the fact that Christians are not the only ones doing youth ministry. We live in a multifaith society. We also looked at the sad statistics that many students and parents are becoming syncretists or nones. But these realities can be good for the church, the Christian family and the Christian youth group in at least two respects. First, it should wake us up to the need to help our own students understand the historic Christian faith, which itself was born in a very crowded religious marketplace. Second, it underscores that theology influences praxis. Our perspective on pluralism affects Christian identity formation. Youth ministries representing the historic faith seem more able to help students flourish spiritually. The early Christians daily dealt with what it meant to be a follower of Christ in a multifaith Greco-Roman culture. There was something noticeably different about their lives, and their message rang true to many of their friends and neighbors. This is why we are in Christian youth ministry. The more we are dwelling "in Christ," the more able we are to help our students live a vital Christianity in our multifaith society.

A few months ago I was pleased to see three high school students new to our youth group playing basketball in our church parking lot with our youth pastor and other students. As their names were called out, I realized these three guys had come regularly to the middle school group three years previous. They had grown so much I hardly recognized them.

These guys were troublemakers in middle school, and all were temporarily banished from youth group (more than once) for bullying or actual physical harm to other students. They usually came back from banishment, but eventually they stopped coming. In middle school they had an interest in the occult and also were attracted to the many positive role models of Muslim black males. Frankly, I assumed they would drop out of high school and eventually be incarcerated.

As the basketball game progressed, one by one they came over to speak with me. They greeted me warmly by my first name. One explained to me that he and another youth group member were going to visit his father, who lived in another city. Why? Having fasted and prayed, he was going to pray with his estranged father that he would be healed from the injuries sustained in a recent car accident.

The second young man explained his interest in social studies in school and envisioned a future of helping people. The third young man explained he was a state championship–level wrestler with plans to attend a university on a wrestling scholarship. He desired to glorify God in the process and help reach others for Christ.

I was dumbfounded.

Normally I am a very positive and hopeful person, but as I said before, in my opinion three years ago these guys had no future other than prison. If religious at all, I figured they would be part of a new age spiritism or identify themselves as Muslim. But now they were Christians, and rather lively ones at that.

I later learned why they disappeared from the youth group. Our church had shrunk in size, and in the process the budget shrank as well. A much-loved youth pastor had to leave to find other ministry employment. The three of them were devastated by this departure. In the years since, our church's student ministry had limped along. Now, though, with a new youth pastor things were picking up and long-lost students were beginning to find their way back.

In our middle school youth group these three guys experienced *presence* and *power*. They experienced amazing grace as well, despite their behavioral failures. Each had led a part of the weekly Bible study. They experienced all of the seven "I am" statements of Jesus as part of this spiritual family.

Subsequent to middle school each of them had experienced significant relational toxicity and numerous family-related setbacks. And yet here they were—godly young men. Not perfect, of course, but on a positive trajectory. In a milieu awash with other choices, they were good examples of what solid Christian identity formation can accomplish.

Student ministry, with presence and power among nones, syncretists and students of other faiths?

In Christ this is mission possible.

APPENDIX 1

Resources Used by Evangelical Free Church Youth Pastors

Though I surveyed only seventy youth pastors of the Evangelical Free Church, the list of resources they use that teach Christ as the only way was quite impressive. The following is a list of some of the resources they used.

VIDEO AND PRINTED CURRICULUM

- AnchorsAway.org, whose tagline is "Community and Resources for Drifting Worldviews," offers curriculum on Christianity and other worldviews.

- Dare2Share.com is a helpful website. It includes "My Life in Six Words" (also available on YouTube at www.youtube.com /watch?v=Ymfh6RJezQ4) and the much-acclaimed "Gospel Journey Maui" (dare2share.org/gospeljourneymaui) a DVD of a "reality *Survivor*–like" program featuring young adults of disparate faith backgrounds. There is considerable tension in this series. It is very real. Additionally there is Dare 2 Share mobile app (dare 2share.org/mobileapp) with help in understanding people of different faiths as well as how to help the Christian faith make sense to them.

- The Gospel Project for Students is a multiweek informational and inspirational curriculum from Lifeway.com that explores biblical theology, missions, Christology and worldview. You will find the Gospel Project at www.lifeway.com/n/Product-Family/The -Gospel-Project/The-Gospel-Project-for-Students.

- SEMP (Summer Evangelistic Missions Program) is a ministry of SonLife, a parachurch organization whose emphasis is discipleship training. See www.sonlife.com for their training/discipleship focus, and www.semp.me for the student portal for this training.

- Simply Youth Ministry's Gospel of John curriculum includes good material on Jesus as the only way. See "The Messiah" at www.sim plyyouthministry.com/resources-curriculum-small-groups-the -messiah.html.

- Summit Ministries (summit.org) offers worldview curriculum and conferences to help students and leaders confidently and positively engage our tolerant cultural.

- Worldview Ministries' materials, featuring speaker Sean Mc-Dowell, are aimed at intellectual skepticism. See the Worldview Ministries website at www.seanmcdowell.org.

BOOKS

- Norman Geisler, Frank Turek and David Limbaugh, *I Don't Have Enough Faith to Be an Atheist* (Wheaton, IL: Crossway, 2004).

- C. S. Lewis, *Mere Christianity* (New York: Macmillan, 1952).

- Dietrich Bonhoeffer, *Life Together* (London: SCM Press, 1954).

YOUTUBE

- Matt Chandler, a young preacher who communicates well with students, offers a four-minute critique of the "Elephant and Blind

Men" analogy, which supports the idea that different religions are each describing God and the world from equally valid perspectives. You can hear Matt's critique at "The Elephant and the Blind Men Contradiction," YouTube, www.youtube.com/watch? v=vTJso93oyKQ.

- Andy Stanley videos on YouTube.com. Search on "Andy Stanley."

- There are many videos on all sides of the issue of religious pluralism on YouTube.com. Search on "Religious Pluralism."

MOVIE

- The movie *Collision*, depicting the true story of good friends, an atheist and a Christian, debating each other in lecture halls around the country. It can be viewed in entirety on YouTube (www .youtube.com/watch?v=cCUmKP4NFKs). For a synopsis and other features, see www.collisionmovie.com.

APPENDIX 2

Protestant Denominations Reviewed in the National Study of Youth and Religion

BLACK PROTESTANT

African Methodist Episcopal Church; African Methodist Episcopal Zion; Christian Methodist Episcopal; National Baptist Convention of America National Baptist Convention, U.S.A. Inc.

CONSERVATIVE PROTESTANT

Adventist; American Baptist; Assemblies of God; Baptist Missionary Association; Bible churches; Calvary Chapel; Charismatic Baptist; charismatic churches; Christian and Missionary Alliance; Christian Reformed Church; Church of Christ; Church of the Brethren; Church of God, General Conference; Church of God of Anderson, Indiana; Church of God of Cleveland, Tennessee; Church of God of Prophesy; Church of God International; Church of the Nazarene; Conservative Baptist Association of America; evangelical churches; Evangelical Covenant Church; Evangelical Free Church; Evangelical Presbyterian Church; Free Will Baptist; Fundamentalist Baptist; fundamentalist churches; General Association of Regular Baptists; General Conference Baptist; Grace Brethren Church; Independent Baptist; independent churches; International Church of the Four-square Gospel; Lutheran Church–Missouri Synod; Mennonite churches; Methodist churches; Missionary Church; North American Baptist; Plymouth Brethren; Presbyterian Church in America; Reformed Presbyterian Churches of North America; Seventh-day Adventist; Southern Baptist Convention; Vineyard Fellowship; Wesleyan Church; Wisconsin Evangelical Lutheran Synod; Worldwide Church of God

MAINLINE PROTESTANT

Congregational Church; Disciples of Christ; Episcopalian Church USA; Evangelical Lutheran Church in America; Moravian Church; Northern Baptist Church; Quakers or Friends; United Brethren in Christ; United Church of Christ; United Methodist Church; Presbyterian Church (USA); Reformed Church in America

NOTES

INTRODUCTION

[1]Sure, I suppose being good on the Xbox is a way to be culturally relevant to youth, and I do use the occasional reference to gaming when I teach the Bible, but, truth be told, I just really enjoy blowing stuff up.

CHAPTER 1: THE RISE OF YOUTH MINISTRY IN OTHER RELIGIONS

[1]Gary Bouma, *Being Faithful in Diversity: Religion and Social Policy in Multifaith Societies* (Adelaide, Australia: ATF Press, 2011), p. 10.

[2]Philip Jenkins, *God's Continent* (Oxford: Oxford University Press, 2007), p. 27.

[3]The most recent United Kingdom census revealed the following regarding religious affiliation: Christians, 59%, no religion, 25%, Muslim, 5%. "2011 Census: Key Statistics for England and Wales, March 2011," Office for National Statistics, accessed March 21, 2013, www.ons.gov.uk/ons/rel/census/2011-census/key-statistics-for-local-authorities-in-england-and-wales/stb-2011-census-key-statistics-for-england-and-wales.html#tab.

[4]The American Religious Identification Survey (ARIS) is conducted by the Institute for the Study of Secularism in Society & Culture, headquartered in Hartford, CT. Good examples of a multisource approach for determining religious affiliation in the United States can be found in the following books: Mark Chaves, *American Religion: Contemporary Trends* (Princeton, NJ: Princeton University Press, 2011); Robert Putnam and Michael Hout, *American Grace: How Religion Divides and Unites Us* (New York: Simon & Schuster, 2012); and Claude Fischer and Michael Hout, *Century of Difference: How America Has Changed in the Last One Hundred Years* (New York: Russell Sage, 2008), p. 186 (see chap. 8).

[5]Michael Mitterauer, *A History of Youth* (Oxford: Blackwell, 1986), p. 18.

[6]This passage always troubled me. It was the first text I studied after I had taken the Hebrew language long enough to ably do Hebrew exegesis. I was relieved to know that there is some exegetical wiggle room in the translation of the term *baqa'* used. For this word, which the KJV renders "tore," the NIV renders "mauled."

[7]A very poignant use of *neotēs* occurs in Acts 20:7-12, where one such young person named Eutychus managed to fall asleep during Paul's all-nighter sermon. He fell out of the upper-floor apartment window and splat onto the pavement below. At least Paul interrupted his message to go bring the kid back to life, after which Paul went right back upstairs and continued preaching till dawn. I like to make the point that the church has been putting kids to sleep ever since, and our role in youth ministry is to help wake up the church to the *na 'arim* and *neotēs* among us.

[8]Mitterauer, *History of Youth*, p. 47.

[9]Susan Davis and Douglas Davis, *Adolescence in a Moroccan Town* (New Brunswick, NJ: Rutgers University Press, 1989), p. 40.

[10]Ibid., pp. 10, 48.

[11]Clifford Geertz, *Local Knowledge: Further Essays in Interpretive Anthropology* (New York: Basic Books, 1983), p. 59. Why are Arab and other non-Western cultures like this? The study of cultural differences was given new vocabulary through the work of Geert Hofstede's "cultural dimensions theory." He posits five dimensions of difference between national cultures. The key measure is the degree to which it is assumed that families and clans will care for one another and put the interests of the group above that of the individual (see Geert Hofstede, *Culture and Organizations: Software of the Mind* [New York, McGraw-Hill, 2004], p. 29; see also Timothy Johnson, "The Relation Between Culture and Response," *Journal of Cross Cultural Psychology* 36, no. 2 [2005]: 264-77). Another way to conceptualize the difference is to think of those cultures that grew out of Greek philosophy and society. Here we find the founding notions in Western society of the emphasis on freedom and the importance of the individual. The Enlightenment in Europe and Middle Ages also, of course, profoundly influenced these same Western societies. Countries that are majority Muslim did not experience the Enlightenment, nor does the etiology of their national consciousness have anything to do with Greek philosophers.

[12]Hans Wehr, *A Dictionary of Modern Literary Arabic* (Ithaca, NY: Cornell University Press, 1966), p. 341.

[13]Davis and Davis, *Adolescence in a Moroccan Town*, p. 51.

[14]Yetkin Yildirim, "Filling Their Hearts with the Love of God: Islamic Perspectives on Spirituality in Childhood and Adolescence," in *Nurturing Child and Adolescent Spirituality*, ed. Karen-Marie Yust et al. (New York: Rowman & Littlefield, 2006), p. 69.

[15]I derived these numbers from a yearlong project of looking up every US mosque on the website salatomatic.com.

[16]I spoke with Muslim youth work leaders in the United States, Canada and the United Kingdom about music, and they all expressed an initial reluctance to use music of any sort. Apparently, conservative (read: "older") Muslim leaders, citing the Qur'an's declaration that all music must glorify Allah, do not feel that Western style music can glorify Allah. Only recently have Muslim youth work leaders decided to take the risk and include bands in their gatherings. (Older Christian youth workers in the United States will remember the "worship wars" of the 1970s and 1980s, where we sometimes feared the reprisal of older church people for daring to use rock music in the context of church youth ministry.)

[17]Aileen Ross, *The Hindu Family in Its Urban Setting* (Toronto: University of Toronto Press, 1961), p. 134.

[18]Vishal Agarwal, "Awakening Latent Spirituality: Nurturing Children in the Hindu Tradition," in Yust, *Nurturing Child and Adolescent Spirituality*, p. 19.

[19]Venkatakrishna B. B. Sastry, "Understanding Dharma, Performing Karma: Shared Responsibilities for Spiritual Grooming in Hindu Traditions," in Yust, *Nurturing Child and Adolescent Spirituality*, p. 368.

[20]"About Us," Hindu Swayamsevak Sangh USA, accessed January 7, 2013, www.hssus .org/content/view/18/112.

[21]"Hindu Temples in the USA," Hindutemples.us, accessed January 7, 2013, www .hindutemples.us.

[22]"HCCC Youth and Education," Shiva-Vishnu Temple, Livermore, accessed January 7, 2013, www.livermoretemple.org/hints/library/temple/hcc_index.asp.

[23]Winston Davis, *Japanese Religion and Society* (Albany, NY: SUNY Press, 1992), p. 15.

[24]For a look at Buddhism from fresh academic eyes see John Harding, ed., *Studying Buddhism in Practice* (London: Routledge, 2011). The contributors concern themselves with practice and norms as opposed to only the tenets of belief.

[25]Yoshiharu Nakagawa, "The Child as Compassionate Dodhisattva and as Human Sufferer/Spiritual Seeker: Intertwined Buddhist Images," in Yust, *Nurturing Child and Adolescent Spirituality*, p. 33.

[26]Sumi Loundon, Ilmee Hwansoo Kim and Benny Liow, "Sunday School for Buddhists? Nurturing Spirituality in Children," in Yust, *Nurturing Child and Adolescent Spirituality*, p. 347.

[27]"Get Involved," Orange County Buddhist Church, accessed January 7, 2013, www .ocbuddhist.org.

[28]"About Nichiren Buddhism," Soka Gakkai International—USA, accessed January 7, 2013, www.facebook.com/SokaGakkaiSgi/posts/196687127142130.

[29]See the website of Soka Gakkai International—USA at www.sgi-usa.org/member resources/zone.php.

[30]Michael Shire, "Learning to Be Righteous: A Jewish Theology of Childhood," in Yust, *Nurturing Child and Adolescent Spirituality*, p. 43.

[31]Jeffry Salkin, "Transforming Bar/Bat Mitzvah: The Role of Family and Community," in Yust, *Nurturing Child and Adolescent Spirituality*, p. 380.

[32]Barry Chazan, "The World of the Jewish Youth Movement," in *The Encyclopedia of Informal Education*, accessed January 7, 2013, www.infed.org/informaljewish education/jewish_youth_movements.htm.

[33]"Jewish Community Service and Organization Locations," BBYO, accessed January 7, 2013, www.bbyo.org.

[34]Homepage, Jewish Students Association, accessed January 7, 2013, www.hbs.edu /mba/student-life/activities-government-and-clubs/Pages/club-details .aspx?name=jewishstudents.

[35]Rational choice theory related to religion began as an analytical tool comparing the state churches of Europe, which are often tax supported, to the United States, where no government funding supports religion. In Europe state churches lose contact with their "customers" because they have no major competition. They have no reason to innovate. America is, by comparison, a different planet, where religions and denominations compete for "customers." The most innovative and those most able to meet the needs of people maintain or increase their market share; the less innovative churches, denominations and religions don't. For a good discussion of rational choice theory as a religion-related analytic framework see Lawrence Young, *Rational Choice Theory and Religion: Summary and Assessment* (New York: Routledge, 1996). For an example of research on church growth expressed in RTC terms, see Paul Pearl and Daniel Olsen, "Religious Market Share and Intensity of Involvement in Five Denominations," *Journal for the Scientific Study of Religion* 39, no. 1 (2000): 12.

CHAPTER 2: THE SCOPE AND NATURE OF MUSLIM YOUTH WORK

[1]Not having any athletic prowess or musical interest, I volunteered weekly in the library of our nearby high school. At the time we had fifty students from our youth group at this school. I loved seeing my students in their natural habitat, and the school allowed me to take a break when the students did so I could meet their friends as well. The school administration knew I was a youth pastor, but that was no concern to them compared to the overwhelming need they had for help in the library.

²Christine Carabain and Rene Bekkers, "Explaining Differences in Philanthropic Behavior Between Christians, Muslims, and Hindus in the Netherlands," *Review of Religious Research* 53, no. 4 (January 2012): 419-40; Khari Brown and Ronald E. Brown, "The Challenge of Religious Pluralism: The Association Between Interfaith Contact and Religious Pluralism," *Review of Religious Research* 53, no. 3 (December 2011): 323-40; Steve Bell and Colin Chapman, eds., *Between Naivety and Hostility: Uncovering the Best Christian Responses of Islam in Britain* (Milton Keynes, UK: Authentic Media, 2011).

³While there is heavy emphasis in Islam on *individual* responsibility toward following the path, it is recognized that prior to puberty a child must be taught, and the right way to live must be modeled, as even the prophet Muhammad did in his own family. See Pamela Taylor, "Personal Responsibility with Communal Support: The Spiritual Education of Muslim Children," in *Nurturing Child and Adolescent Spirituality*, ed. Karen-Marie Yust et al. (Oxford: Rowman & Littlefield, 2006), pp. 352-65.

⁴See this concern in the United States in Marcia Hermansen and Shabana Mir's "Identity Jihads: The Multiple Strivings of American Muslim Youth," in Yust, *Nurturing Child and Adolescent Spirituality*, pp. 423-36.

⁵Christian Smith et al., *American Evangelicalism: Embattled and Thriving* (Chicago: University of Chicago Press, 1998).

⁶Ibid., pp. 118-19. See also a more general analysis of youth culture by Mike Brake, *Comparative Youth Culture: The Sociology of Youth Cultures and Youth Subcultures in America, Britain, and Canada* (New York: Routledge, 1990).

⁷Joyce Marie Mushaben, "Gender, HipHop and Pop-Islam: the Urban Identities of Muslim Youth in Germany," *Citizenship Studies* 12, no. 5 (October 2008): 507-26.

⁸John Bolby, "The Making and Breaking of Affectional Bonds: Etiology and Psychopathology in the Light of Attachment Theory," *British Journal of Psychiatry* 130 (January 1977): 201-10.

⁹Lee Kirkpatrick, "An Attachment-Theory Approach to Psychology of Religion," *International Journal for the Psychology of Religion* 2, no. 1 (1992): 3-28; Marjorie Gunnoe and Kristin Moore, "Predictors of Religiosity Among Youth Aged 17-22," *Journal for the Scientific Study of Religion* 41, no. 4 (December 2002): 613-22.

¹⁰Mieke Maliepaard, Marcel Lubbers and Merove Gisberts, "Generational Differences in Ethnic and Religious Attachment and Their Interrelations: A Study Among Muslim Minorities in the Netherlands," *Ethnic and Racial Studies* 33, no. 3 (January 2010): 451-72.

¹¹Peter Granqvist, "Attachment Theory and Religious Conversions: A Review and

a Resolution of the Classic and Contemporary Paradigm Chasm," *Review of Religious Research* 45, no. 2 (December 2003): 172-87.

[12]For a good example of this research in the United States, see Christian Smith and Melinda Denton, *Soul Searching: The Religious and Spiritual Lives of American Teenagers* (New York: Oxford University Press, 2005). This is the first of several book-length publications stemming from the National Study of Youth and Religion.

[13]David Dollahite et al., "Giving Up Something Good for Something Better: Sacred Sacrifices Made by Religious Youth," *Journal of Adolescent Research* 24, no. 6 (November 2009): 691-720. See also a study out of Lebanon by Lillian Ghandour, Elie Karam and Wadih Maalouf, "Lifetime Alcohol Use, Abuse and Dependence Among University Students in Lebanon: Exploring the Role of Religiosity in Different Faiths," *Addiction* 104, no. 6 (June 2009): 940-48.

[14]Mark Grey, "Muslim Religiosity and Personality Development Index," *Review of Religious Research* 46, no. 4 (June 2004): 422-26. See also a study of religiosity and moral development in Muslim youth by Steven Krauss et al., "Exploring Regional Differences in Religiosity Among Muslim Youth in Malaysia," *Review of Religious Research* 47, no. 3 (March 2006): 238-52.

[15]My thanks to Nyack College students Anna Bailey and Tom Belo for their tireless and exacting work in creating Excel files with key information on these mosques. While the information currency or correctness of each mosque listed was not verified in this research, the comprehensive nature of salatomatic.com provides at least a starting point when it comes to key information.

[16]"MAS Youth Houston," Muslim American Society Houston, accessed December 3, 2013, www.mashouston.org/DEPARTMENTS/Youth.aspx.

[17]"Mission Statement," Muslim Youth Camp of California, accessed June 21, 2012, http://muslimyouthcamp.org.

[18]"Services," BC Muslim Association, accessed June 21, 2012, http://thebcma.com/#.

[19]"Courses," Muslim Youth Skills, accessed June 21, 2012, www.muslimyouthskills.co.uk/courses.

[20]"About Us," Muslim Youth Skills, accessed June 21, 2012, www.muslimyouthskills.co.uk/about.

[21]"Programs in Canada," Muslim Assocation of Canada, accessed December 3, 2013, www.macnet.ca/English/Pages/Programs-in-Canada.aspx?SubDepartment=Youth9629Programs.

[22]See Muslim Youth of North America website at http://myna.org.

[23]"The Straight Path Initiative," Muslim American Society, accessed December 3, 2013, www.muslimamericansociety.org/main/content/straight-path-initiative.

[24]Homepage, Muslim Youthwork Foundation, accessed July 2, 2012, http://mywf.org.uk.

[25]Andrew Root and Kenda Creasy Dean, *The Theological Turn in Youth Ministry* (Downers Grove, IL: InterVarsity Press, 2011); Tony Jones, *The Church Is Flat: The Relational Ecclesiology of the Emerging Church Movement* (Minneapolis: JoPa Group, 2011); and Pete Ward, *Perspectives on Ecclesiology and Ethnography* (Grand Rapids: Eerdmans, 2012).

[26]Brian Belton and Sadek Hamid, eds., *Youth Work and Islam: A Growing Tradition* (Rotterdam: Sense Publishers, 2011), p. 6.

[27]"*Ilm*," Islamicdictionary.com, accessed July 2, 2012, www.islamic-dictionary.com/index.php?word=ilm.

[28]Frederick Denny, "The Meaning of 'Ummah' in the Qur'an," *History of Religions* 15, no. 1 (August 1975): 34-70.

[29]For example, see Muhammad Anwar, "Religious Identity in Plural Societies: The Case of Britain," *Journal of the Institute of Muslim Minority Affairs* 2, no. 2 (1980): 110-21.

[30]Tahir Alam, "Enhancing Youth Work Practice Through the Concepts of Islamic Morality and Education," in Belton and Hamid, *Youth Work and Islam*, p. 30.

[31]Maurice Irfan Coles, "Every Muslim Youth Matters: The 4 Ps of Muslim Participation," in Belton and Hamid, *Youth Work and Islam*, pp. 102-3.

[32]It will be helpful to readers outside the United Kingdom to understand there is a vast "community youth work" infrastructure in the United Kingdom. Universities offer degrees in "youth and community youth work" and, until the budget cuts of 2010–2011, virtually every village, town and city had at least one paid full-time youth worker who maintained community-based programs and events to service the needs especially of minority or economically disadvantaged youth.

[33]Jonathan Roberts, "Making a Place for Muslim Youth Work in British Youth Work," *Youth and Policy* 92 (summer 2006): 28.

[34]For example, see Leon Feinstein, John Bynner and Kathryn Duckworth, "Leisure Contexts and Adolescents and Their Effects on Adult Outcomes," *Journal of Youth Studies* 9, no. 3 (2006): 305-27; and L. Platt, *Migration and Social Mobility: The Life Chances of Britain's Minority Ethnic Communities* (York: Joseph Rowntree Foundation, 2005). Particularly poignant is Thomas Wylie, "An Opportunity Wasted," *Young People Now* 7 (December 2005): 23.

[35]Ask What If, accessed July 9, 2012, www.askwhatif.co.uk/wp-content/uploads/community-worker.pdf.

[36]For a more complete list see S. Gilliant, "A Descriptive Account of Islamic Youth Organizations in the UK," *American Journal of Islamic Social Sciences* (fall 1996).

[37]See the Muslim Youth Helpline website at www.myh.org.uk.

[38]Brian Belton, "Youth Work and Islam: A Growing Tradition," in Belton and Hamid, *Youth Work and Islam*, p. 18.

[39]See, for example, the Muslim Scouts of Michigan homepage at www.themuslim scouts.com.

[40]"MFNS Big Brothers & Big Sisters," Society Muslim Families Network, accessed November 13, 2013, www.muslimfamiliesnetwork.org/big-sister-big-brother/.

[41]"Ayal Muslim Youth Help Line," British Columbia Muslims, accessed November 13, 2013, http://bcmuslims.com/organization/ayal-muslim-youth-help-line.html.

CHAPTER 3: THE RISE OF SYNCRETISTS AND NONES

[1]Barry Kosmin and Ariela Keysar, "American Nones: The Profile of the No Religion Population, A Report Based on the American Religious Identification Survey 2008" (Hartford: Trinity College, 2008), pp. 14, 17, 20, accessed January 12, 2013, http://commons.trincoll.edu/aris/files/2011/08/NONES_08.pdf. Among the many other fascinating findings is the state-by-state ranking of nones as a percentage of the state population. Vermont is first with 34%, and Mississippi has the smallest with 5%. A more detailed analysis of the move toward nones can be found in Michael Hout and Claude Fisher, "Why More Americans Have No Religious Preference," *American Sociological Review* 67, no. 2 (2002): 165-90. Contrary to the dire forecasts of increasing secularization in the United States and globally comes John Micklethwait and Adrian Wooldridge, *God Is Back: How the Global Revival of Faith Is Changing the World* (New York: Penguin, 2009), which highlights that vital and living religious faith is surging around the world, especially among the educated.

[2]Christian Smith and Patricia Snell, *Souls in Transition: The Religious and Spiritual Lives of Emerging Adults in America* (New York: Oxford University Press, 2009), p. 95.

[3]Ibid., p. 168.

[4]Ibid., p. 84.

[5]For example, see Richard Caputo, "Parent Religiosity, Family Processes, and Adolescent Outcomes," *Families in Society* 85, no. 4 (2004): 495-510. Another good example is Jiexia Zhai and Charles Stoke, "Ethnic and Family Social Contextual Influences on Asian American Adolescent Religiosity," *Sociological Spectrum* 29, no. 2 (2009): 201.

[6]Two fascinating examples are Annie Wertz and Timson German, "Belief-Desire Reasoning in the Explanation of Behavior: Do Actions Speaker Louder Than Words?" *Cognition* 105, no. 1 (2007): 184-94; and Marie Cornwell, "The Determi-

nants of Religious Behavior: A Theoretical Model and Empirical Test," *Social Forces* 68, no. 2 (1989): 572-92.

[7]David Kinnaman, *You Lost Me: Why Young Christians Are Leaving Church and Rethinking Church* (Grand Rapids: Baker, 2011). His follow-up book, *UnChristian: What a New Generation Really Thinks About Christianity and Why It Matters* (Grand Rapids Baker, 2012), classifies emerging adults (aside from the 30% in their research who were active in their faith as high school students and remained so in their twenties) as *prodigals* (12%), who have lost their faith, *nomads* (40%), who identify themselves as Christians but have stepped away from church for a variety of reasons, and *exiles* (18%), who have left the church because they cannot reconcile "church culture" with the real culture they live in.

[8]Neuroscience is now documenting the long-term effects of early emotional toxicity in the home. The effect in adolescents from early childhood emotional trauma include regulating emotions, attention deficit, negative academic performance, poor health, diminished ability to form social bonds, and depression. It behooves youth workers to care about the health of their youth group members' parents' marriage. For a good introduction see John Medina, *Brain Rules: 12 Principles for Surviving and Thriving at Work, Home and School* (Seattle: Pear Press, 2008), pp. 172-94. See especially Brain Rule 8: "Stressed brains do not learn the same way as non-stressed brains."

[9]"Overview," Recovering from Religion, accessed November 13, 2013, http://recoveringfromreligion.org/about/overview/.

[10]Ibid.

[11]A look at the list of sponsors illustrates well the none world: American Atheists, American Humanist Association, Atheist Alliance of America, Atheist Nexus, Camp Quest, Center for Inquiry, Foundation Beyond Belief, Freedom from Religion Foundation, Freethought Society, Military Association of Atheists and Freethinkers, National Atheist Party, Secular Coalition for America, Secular Student Alliance, Society for Humanistic Judaism, Stiefel Freethought Foundation, the Brights, the James Rani Educational Foundation, the Richard Dawkins Foundation, United Coalition of Reason, and the Washington Area Secular Humanists. For an academic study of organizations in the United States particularly for atheists see Jesse Smith, "Creating a Godless Community: The Collective Identity Work of Contemporary American Atheists," *Journal for the Scientific Study of Religion* 52, no. 1 (2013): 80-99.

[12]"Affiliated Campus Group List," Secular Student Alliance, accessed February 13, 2013, http://secularstudents.org/affiliates.

[13]There is a daily devotional for nones: Joe C., *Beyond Belief: Agnostic Musings for 12 Step Life* (Toronto: Rebellion Dogs, 2013).

[14]See Nicholas Babchuk and Hugh Whitt, "R-Order and Religious Switching," *Journal for the Scientific Study of Religion* 29, no. 2 (June 1990): 246-55.

[15]Christian Smith and Patrice Snell, *Souls in Transition: The Religious and Spiritual Lives of Emerging Adults in America* (New York: Oxford University Press, 2009), p. 104.

[16]Ibid., p. 137.

[17]Mike Nappa, *The Jesus Survey* (Grand Rapids: Baker Books, 2012). The Jesus Survey did not use national random sampling techniques but rather surveyed the workers of their 2010 camps. Nappa does not claim his statistics represent all US young people or even all US Christian young people. His survey speaks only of those he surveyed. Having said that, however, it is important to note these young people, the cream of the crop spiritually, came from twenty different conservative and mainline denominations. If the Jesus Survey results speak of only the very brightest and best, many will agree with Nappa that the story is not good if one holds to the traditional/historic Christian perspective.

[18]I have some reservations about certain aspects of the Jesus Survey. Specifically, it seems to ignore the cognitive development issues when it comes to asking questions about faith. For example, how many seventh-grade boys would have been listening in church or youth group when the concept of Jesus as God was explained to them? I have my doubts. Nonetheless, the denominational differences are quite dramatic, even given the caveat of early adolescent cognitive development.

[19]Christian Smith and Melinda Denton, *Soul Searching: The Religious and Spiritual Lives of American Teenagers* (New York: Oxford University Press, 2005), p. 160. The retreat of religion in the public square and its relegation exclusively to the private realm has been addressed poignantly in Stephen Carter, *The Cultural of Disbelief* (New York: Basic Books, 1993). The fault lines in public opinion about subjects that had broad social consensus appeared with the rise of tolerance education. An early and critically acclaimed effort to describe this fracturing is James Davidson Hunter, *Culture Wars: The Struggle to Control the Family, Art, Education, Law, and Politics in America* (New York: Basic Books, 1991).

[20]Nappa, *Jesus Survey*, p. 73.

[21]Smith and Denton, *Soul Searching*, p. 161.

[22]Smith and Snell, *Souls in Transition*, p. 45.

[23]Jürgen Habermas, *The Theory of Communicative Action* (Boston: Beacon, 1987). A broader background can be gained by reading Michael Foucault, *The Archaeology*

of Knowledge (New York, Pantheon, 1972); and Talcott Parson, *Action Theory and the Human Condition* (New York: Free Press, 1978).

[24]Smith and Snell, *Souls in Transition*, p. 75.

[25]A typical example is Charles Arn, "5 Top Priorities for Increasing Your Church," accessed November, 13, 2013, www.sermoncentral.com/pastors-preaching-articles/charles-arn-5-top-priorities-for-increasing-your-church-753.asp.

[26]For example, see Terrance Hicks and Samuel Heistie, "High School to College Transition: A Profile of the Stressors, Physical and Psychological Health Issues That Affect the First Year on Campus College Student," *Journal of Cultural Diversity* 15, no. 3 (Fall 2008): 143-47. Knowing a person of another faith is likely to increase positive attitudes toward that faith. This can be seen in Robert Putnam and David Campbell, *American Grace: How Religion Divides and Unites Us* (New York: Simon & Schuster, 2010), and the publication by the Pew Forum on Religious and Public Life, 2009 Annual Religion and Public Life Survey, "Views of Religious Similarities and Differences: Muslims Widely Seen as Facing Discrimination," November 24, 2012, www.pewforum.org/files/2009/09/survey0909.pdf. Yet another study is Ronald Brown, "The Challenge of Religious Pluralism: The Association Between Interfaith Contact and Religious Pluralism," *Review of Religious Research* 53, no. 3 (2011): 323-40.

[27]First put forward as a theory in 1993, see a more recent work by Roger Fink and Rodney Stark, *The Churching of America: Winners and Losers in Our Religious Economy, 1776–2005* (New Brunswick, NJ: Rutgers University Press, 2005). An excellent example of rational choice theory applied is by Darren Sherkat and John Wilson, "Preferences, Constraints, and Choices in Religious Markets: An Examination of Religious Switching and Apostasy," *Social Forces* 73, no. 3 (1995): 993-1026.

[28]See John Micklethwait's *God Is Back: How the Global Revival of Faith Is Changing the World* (New York: Penguin, 2009).

[29]The Pew Forum on Religion and Public Life, "Faith in Flux: Changes in Religious Affiliation in American Religious Life" (Washington DC: Pew Research Center, 2009).

[30]Leonard Kageler, "High School Youth Groups: Growth and Decline," PhD diss. (Fordham University, 1999). The aptness of rational choice is certainly evident when we explore Muslim-to-Muslim youth ministry.

[31]"The evil spirit answered them, 'Jesus I know, and I know about Paul, but who are you'? Then the man who had the evil spirit jumped on them and overpowered them all. He gave them such a beating that they ran out of the house naked and bleeding" (Acts 19:15-16).

[32]Smith and Denton, *Soul Searching*, pp. 162-63.

[33]Ibid., p. 166.

[34]"The Apostles' Creed," *Creeds.net*, accessed March 14, 2013, www.creeds.net/ancient/apostles.htm.

[35]"The Nicene Creed," *Creeds.net*, accessed March 14, 2013, www.creeds.net/ancient/nicene.htm.

[36]"Westminster Confession of Faith," Center for Reformed Theology and Apologetics, accessed March 14, 2013, www.reformed.org/documents/wcf_with_proofs.

[37]For a book-length treatment see Andrew Murray and John Flavel, *The Believer's Prophet, Priest and King* (Ada, MI: Bethany House, 1989).

[38]"What Do We Believe?" *The Alliance*, accessed December 15, 2012, www.cmalliance.org/about/beliefs.

[39]A good explanation of this view of Christ can be had in William Bellinger and William Farmer, *Jesus and the Suffering Servant* (New York: Continuum, 1998). A more comprehensive discussion is aptly presented in Darrell Bock and Mitch Glaser, *The Gospel According to Isaiah 53: Encountering the Suffering Servant in Jewish and Christian Theology* (Grand Rapids: Kregel Academic, 2012).

[40]An example of a discussion of the incarnation that does not focus on "one way" is Andrew Root's *Revisiting Relational Youth Ministry*. His chapter "Who Is Jesus Christ?" is an excellent and fresh expression of Christology that aims to help the youth worker re-present Christ more fully in the ministry of "place sharing." See Andrew Root, *Revisiting Relational Youth Ministry* (Downers Grove, IL: InterVarsity Press, 2007), pp. 85-103.

[41]Alaine de Boton, *Religion For Atheists* (New York: Random House, 2012), p. 12. While reading his book I wondered if he had read any of the NSYR research. It is certainly possible.

CHAPTER 4: CHRISTIANS IN OCCUPIED TERRITORY

[1]Sarah Iles Johnston, *Religions of the Ancient World: A Guide* (Cambridge, MA: Belknap, 2004), p. 399.

[2]Geraldine Finch, *Egyptian Mythology: A Guide to the Gods, Goddesses, and Traditions of Ancient Egypt* (New York: Oxford University Press, 2004), pp. 99-115.

[3]Lev 18:21; 20:2-5 are especially telling. What kind of personal crises or issues would cause parents to consider sacrificing one or more of their own children to Molek? That this was an actual possibility is shown by the author of Leviticus specifically warning the Hebrews against it.

[4]Perhaps this is akin to Christian parents naming their children after Bible heroes,

or Muslim parents including Muhammad as part of the given name for a son.

[5]This rectangular box contained the two stone tables on which the Ten Commandments were written. The notion of using the weaponization of the Ark will be recalled by some as the reason the Nazis wanted the Ark in the first Indiana Jones movie.

[6]A representative sample of these scholars' books includes Wayne A. Meeks, *The First Urban Christians: The Social World of the Apostle Paul* by (Hartford, CT: Yale University Press, 2003); Larry Hurtado, *Lord Jesus Christ: Devotion to Jesus in Earliest Christianity* (Grand Rapids: Eerdmans, 2005); Todd Still and David Horrell, *After the First Urban Christians: The Social Scientific Study of Pauline Christianity* (Charlottesville: University of Virginia Press, 2009). See also an earlier but excellent work by Philip Esler, *The First Christians in Their Social World: Social-Scientific Approaches to New Testament Interpretation* (New York: Routledge, 1994).

[7]One of my favorite and most poignant examples of Roman world mail comes from the Roman fort on Hadrian's Wall in Northern England. Archaeologists have discovered that the fort threw its waste paper in the fort's latrines. Apparently urine helps preserve parchment, as thousands of documents have been unearthed. These include troop rosters, equipment inventories and the like, but also letters. My two favorites: first from a mother in Italy, "Dear Son, did you receive the socks and underwear I sent you?" and from a nearby fort commander's wife to the wife of the commander at Vindolanda, "You are invited to my birthday party, which will be held ten days hence." A good representative of the many books on this fascinating site is Robin Birley, *Vindolanda* (Stroud, UK: Amberley, 2009).

[8]Robin Lane Fox, *Pagans and Christians* (San Francisco: HarperCollins, 1998), contains primary sources, which are quoted extensively.

[9]See Philip A. Harlan, *Dynamics of Identity in the World of the Early Christians* (London: T & T Clark, 2009). A good summary can be found at www.philipharland .com/Blog/2007/11/09/breaking-news-early-christians-were-impious-atheists/.

[10]See Herodotus, *Histories*, bk. 1, chap. 99, www.perseus.tufts.edu/hopper /searchresults?target=en&all_words=Aphrodite&phrase=and+have+intercours e&any_words=&exclude_words=&documents.

[11]Rodney Stark, *The Rise of Christianity: How the Obscure, Marginal Jesus Movement Became the Dominant Religious Force in the Western World in a Few Centuries* (New York: Harper, 1997). This book was updated in under the title *The Triumph of Christianity: How the Jesus Movement Became the World's Largest Religion* (New York: Harper, 2011).

[12]A well-documented example of a Christian facing death with a smile is Polycarp,

who was the head of the church in Smyrna. In front of thousands of people, he was given the opportunity to renounce Christianity by turning toward a group of imprisoned Christians also about to be killed and saying "Away with the atheists." (Romans considered Christians atheists because they did not believe in the Roman pantheon of gods.) Polycarp said, in effect, "No thanks," and then, with a smile, turned toward the Roman leaders and said the words "Away with the atheists!" That did it, and immediately he was tethered and the fire lit. To stop his singing and preaching they speared him. See J. B. Lightfoot, *The Martyrdom of Polycarp* (Seattle: Amazon Digital, 2010).

[13]Charles Schmidt, *The Social Results of Early Christianity* (Whitefish, MO: Kessinger, 2007), p. 293. Note Emperor Julian's referring to Christians as "impious." That is, Christians only believed in one God, not the Roman pantheon.

[14]Christian Smith and Melinda Denton, *Soul Searching: The Religious and Spiritual Lives of American Teenagers* (New York: Oxford University Press, 2005), p. 158.

[15]Ibid., pp. 159-61.

[16]See Christian Smith and Patricia Snell, *Souls in Transition* (New York: Oxford University Press, 2009), a five-year follow-up of the original study. Kenda Dean, *Almost Christian* (New York: Oxford University Press, 2010) is an attempt to help churches find a way out of being producers of moralistic therapeutic deists. Christian Smith et al., *Lost in Transition* (New York: Oxford University Press, 2011) focuses on the many 18- to 23-year-olds who are seemingly lost, filling their lives with consumerism, intoxication, risky sexual practices and civil apathy.

CHAPTER 5: THEOLOGY IN PRAXIS

[1]The term *mainline* refers to many of the early American Protestant denominations that became theologically liberal over time. (The etiology of the term itself probably refers to the nineteenth-century "main" railroad lines radiating out from the centers of cities on the Eastern seaboard. These denominations were quick to establish churches in these new cities along the main railroad line.) One of the first well-known research-based books about outcomes based on theology was Dean Kelly, *Why Conservative Churches Are Growing* (Macon, GA: Mercer University Press, 1972). Kelly documented the precipitous decline in membership and attendance in liberal denominations in the 1950s to the early 1970s compared to the accelerating numerical growth in evangelical and conservative denominations.

[2]A good example of this is the Episcopal Church of the Good Samaritan in Paoli, a western suburb of Philadelphia. Their website proclaims, "We are an active Episcopal church committed to spreading the Gospel of Jesus Christ." Their youth

ministry is described as, "Each part of the ministry works together to provide life-changing lessons and experiences, helping students grow into a closer relationship with Jesus Christ. We want to see our teenagers to become men and women of God—becoming leaders in their schools and communities. We believe that an authentic faith is a faith that effects every area of our lives. In this ministry, we do our best to help guide teenagers into living that out." Homepage and "Welcome to Good Sam Youth Ministries," Church of the Good Samaritan, www .good-Samaritan.org and www.good-samaritan.org/youth.

[3]See appendix 2 for the full list.

[4]Subsequent to the release of *Soul Searching*, some liberal denominations have responded aggressively to upgrade their youth ministry programs. For example, I met one denominational official at a conference in Seattle who was in charge of a district of his denominational churches in the western United States. His "head office" authorized him to find ten quality evangelical youth pastors to place in district churches and offer them each a salary package of $100,000 per year.

[5]I would expect that if the NSYR were conducted today, Roman Catholic youth would score high in many aspects of religiosity. There is a backstory to this expectation. A few years before the NSYR, US Catholic bishops completely rewrote their mission and vision for Roman Catholic youth ministry. In many respects it is similar to conservative Protestant statements in its concern for salvation, discipleship and personal spiritual formation. See US Catholic Bishops, "Renewing the Vision: A framework for Catholic Youth Ministry," *Origins* 27, no. 9 (July 1997), available online at www.usccb.org/about/laity-marriage-family-life-and -youth/young-adults/renewing-the-vision.cfm. Now Roman Catholic youth ministry has a much larger emphasis in churches. This high priority of youth ministry is supported by The National Federation for Catholic Youth Ministries, which now provides a full suite of services for the five thousand-plus full-time US Roman Catholic youth workers along with their volunteers.

[6]Patricia Snell et al., "Denominational Differences in Congregational Youth Ministry Programs and Evidence of Systematic Non-Response Biases," *Review of Religious Research* 51, no. 1 (September 2009): 21-38.

[7]"Research Notes," *Review of Religious Research* 44, no. 3 (2003): 301-16.

[8]Gary Goreham, "Denominational Comparisons of Rural Youth Ministry Programs," *Review of Religious Research* 45, no. 4 (June 2004): 336-48.

[9]Steven Tigue, "Protestant Adolescent Socialization and Denominational Growth," *Journal of Youth Ministry* 10, no. 2 (spring 2012): 43-62.

[10]Andrew Singleton, Ruth Webber, Joyce Mari and Dorissa Arrigo, "The Practice of

Youth Ministry in a Changing Context: Results from Australian Scoping Study," *Journal of Youth Ministry* 9, no. 1 (fall 2010): 35-54.

[11]See Donald Bridge and David Phypers, *The Waters That Divide: Two View of Baptism Explored* (Fearn, UK: Christian Focus, 2008).

[12]Some of my European colleagues tell me that in their communities it is considered improper to have outreach events, since virtually everyone is baptized as an infant and therefore all are saved and already thus connected to a baptizing congregation. For one youth group to invite other youth to their church activities is akin to sheep stealing!

[13]A robust apologetic for the traditional view can be found in Harold Netland, *Encountering Religious Pluralism: The Challenge to Christian Faith and Mission* (Downers Grove, IL: IVP Academic, 2001). An earlier contribution to discourse on pluralism is Lesslie Newbigin, *The Gospel in a Pluralist Society* (Grand Rapids: Eerdmans, 1989). I especially like his distinction between knowing and believing: "I have suggested that there is an error in the frequently repeated statement that we live in a pluralist society. We are pluralist in respect of what we call beliefs, but we are not pluralist in respect of what we call facts" (ibid., p. 27).

[14]Many traditional student ministries similarly use mission or purpose statements. Among the main paradigms are the "Sonlife" strategy and the "purpose-driven" strategy. In the Sonlife strategy a youth ministry is modeled after the pattern of ministry of Jesus in the Gospels: outreach, spiritual growth, ministry training and leadership (see www.sonlife.com). Purpose-driven youth ministry anchors student ministry in the fivefold purposes of the early church, which are found in the opening chapters of the book of Acts: evangelism, teaching, fellowship, worship and service. See Doug Field, *Purpose-Driven Youth Ministry* (Grand Rapids: Zondervan, 1998).

[15]See John Paul II, "Redemptoris Missio," The Holy See, accessed November 2, 2012, www.vatican.va/edocs/ENG0219/_INDEX.HTM.

[16]Jacques Dupuis, *Toward a Christian Theology of Religious Pluralism* (Maryknoll, NY: Orbis, 2002). An example of a serious evangelical work on pluralism is Netland, *Encountering Religious Pluralism.*

[17]Depuis, *Toward a Christian Theology of Religious Pluralism*, p. 285.

[18]Ibid., pp. 292-93.

[19]"This Is Who We Are," First Congregational Church of Glen Ellyn, accessed October 20, 2012, http://fccge.org/content/discover/about-fccge.

[20]Rachel Bahr, phone interview by the author, March 18, 2013.

[21]Ibid.

[22]Ibid.

[23]Ibid.

[24]Homepage, University Congregational United Church of Christ, accessed March 10, 2013, www.universityucc.org.

[25]"Youth Ministry Program at University Congregational, Grades 6-12," www.universityucc.org/education/youthed.htm.

[26]Margaret Irribarra, phone interview by author, March 18, 2013.

[27]Mary Hess, "Following Christ in a Web 2.0 World: Moving from Sympathy to Empathy," 15th Annual Forum of the Association of Youth Ministry Educators, Louisville, KY, October 18, 2009.

[28]"Pluralistic Monotheism and the Abrahamic Faiths," Harford Seminary, fall 2008.

[29]See John Hick, *The Metaphor of God Incarnate: Christology in a Pluralistic Age*, 2nd ed. (Westminster John Knox, 2006).

[30]Keith Johnson, "John Hick's Pluralistic Hypothesis and the Problem of Conflicting Truth-Claims," 1997, www.leaderu.com/theology/hick.html.

[31]There are book-length treatments of Hick's approach to pluralism. See Adnan Asian, *Religious Pluralism in Christian and Islamic Philosophy: The Thought of John Hick and Seyyed Hossein Nasr* (New York: Routledge, 1998); and Heather Meacock, *An Anthropological Approach to Theology: A Study of John Hick's Theology of Religious Pluralism, Towards Ethical Criteria for a Global Theology of Religions* (Lanham, MD: University Press of America, 2000). A good summary is found in S. Mark Heim's *Salvations: Truth and Difference in Religion* (Maryknoll, NY: Orbis, 1995), p. 13.

[32]"Colonize my life world" comes out of the sociological theory of Talcott Parsons and Jürgen Habermas. Their work provides rich vocabulary for the foundations and outworking of postmodernism. See Talcott Parsons, *The Structure of Social Action*, 2. vols. (New York: Simon & Schuster, 1967); and Jürgen Habermas and Thomas McCarthy, *Theory of Communicative Action* (Boston: Beacon, 1985).

[33]Bob Smietana, "Unitarian Faith Growing Nationwide," *Blue Boat*, October 2, 2012, http://blueboat.blogs.uua.org/soundings/growing-in-faith/.

[34]"Youth Ministry," Unitarian Universalist Association of Congregations, accessed October 3, 2012, www.uua.org/re/youth/index.shtml.

[35]"Tapestry of Faith Programs for Youth," Unitarian Universalist Association of Congregations, accessed October 17, 2012, www.uua.org/re/tapestry/youth/index.shtml.

[36]Eboo Patel, ed., *Building the Interfaith Youth Movement: Beyond Dialogue to Action* (Lanham, MD: Rowman & Littlefield, 2006) p. 15. See also pp. 257-62.

[37]I find it so interesting, however, that Heim considers himself an evangelical Christian. One way to understand his project is that he is creating space for beliefs in a marketplace that would otherwise be hostile.

[38]John Cobb and Paul Knitter, *Transforming Christianity and the World: A Way Beyond Absolutism and Relativism* (Maryknoll, NY: Orbis, 1999), p. 95.

[39]Ibid., p. 102.

CHAPTER 6: MULTIFAITH PERSPECTIVES

[1]The movie *Trainspotting* aptly depicts 1980s heroin-fogged young people subsisting in urban poverty and squalor in the country in question. (Note: this is *not* a movie for youth group night.)

[2]The research was deepened and extended over the years. A good book-length treatment of the Teenage and Religion Values Survey is Leslie J. Francis, William Kay, Alan Kerbey and Olaf Fogwill, eds., *Fast Moving Currents in Youth Culture* (Oxford: Lynx Communication, 1995). An excellent presentation of the study design and ongoing nature of the Teenage Religion and Values Survey is Mandy Robbins and Leslie J. Francis, "The Teenage Religion and Values Survey in England and Wales: An Overview," *British Journal of Religious Education* 32, no. 3 (September 2010): 307-20.

[3]See part 1, chapters 1 and 6-9 of "Education Reform Act 1988," The National Archives, accessed January 9, 2013, www.legislation.gov.uk/ukpga/1988/40/contents.

[4]C. S. Lewis, *Surprised by Joy* (New York: Harcourt, Brace, 1955), p. 228.

[5]Peter Berger, *The Sacred Canopy* (New York: Doubleday, 1967). See especially chap. 6, "Secularization and the Problem of Plausibility" (pp. 126-53). Thirty years later he writes about his 180-degree opinion change: "Let me repeat what I said awhile back: The world today is massively religious, is anything but the secularized world that had been predicted (whether joyfully or despondently) by so many analysts of modernity" (*The Descularization of the World* [Grand Rapids: Eerdmans, 1999], p. 9).

[6]Rodney Stark, interview with the author, December 8, 2004.

[7]Comparing religiosity across different religions is still new. Almost all social science research about youth religiosity in North America and the United Kingdom has focused on youth religiosity in terms of the Christian faith. It is not that teenagers of other religions have not shown up in some studies, but their numbers are so small that conclusions about the "protective effects" of religiosity are not warranted. Some good studies have come out of Malaysia, but it is of Muslims only. Some studies have bemoaned the difficulty in doing truly multire-

ligious research. One attempt, for example, included a Likert Scale response item to the statement "When I am disconnected from the spiritual dimension of my life, I lose my sense of purpose." The researchers found Jewish and Muslim students completely uncomprehending (see Devon Berry et al., "Measuring Religiosity in Diverse Religious Groups: A Consideration of Methods," *Journal of Religion and Health* 50 [January 2011]: 841-51).

[8]Sam Hardy and Marcela Raffaelli, "Adolescent Religiosity and Sexuality," *Journal of Adolescence* 26, no. 7 (2003): 731-40. A different research approach mining the same data set by University of Wisconsin sociologist Ann Meier corroborated results. See Ann Meier, "Adolescent Transition to First Intercourse, Religiosity and Attitudes About Sex," *Social Forces* 81, no. 5 (2003): 1031-52.

[9]James Nonnemaker, Clea McNeely and Robert Blum, "Public and Private Domains of Religiosity and Adolescent Health Risk Behaviors: Evidence from the National Longitudinal Study of Adolescent Health," *Social Science and Medicine* 57, no. 11 (2003): 2049-55.

[10]Stephen Leibowitz, Dolores Castellano and Israel Cuellar, "Factors That Predict Sexual Behavior Among Young Mexican American Adolescents," *Hispanic Journal of Behavioral Sciences* 21, no. 4 (1999): 470-570.

[11]S. Rostosky, B. Wilcox, M. Wright and B. Randall, "The Impact of Religiosity on Adolescent Sexual Behavior: A Review of the Evidence," *Journal of Adolescent Research* 19, no. 6 (2004): 677.

[12]Shawnika Hull et al., "Identifying the Causal Pathways from Religiosity to Delayed Adolescent Sexual Behavior," *Journal of Sex Research* 48, no. 6 (2011): 543-53.

[13]Richard Fehring, Kerry Cheever, Kart German and Connie Philpot, "Religiosity and Sexual Activity Among Older Adolescents," *Journal of Religion and Health* 37, no. 3 (1998): 229-49.

[14]Lawrence Nicholas, "The Association Between Religiosity, Sexual Fantasy, Participation Sexual Acts, Sexual Enjoyment, Exposure and Reaction to Sexual Materials Among Black South African Youth," *Journal of Sex and Marital Therapy* 30 (2004): 37-42.

[15]Chris Stewart and John Bollard, "Parental Style as Possible Mediator of the Relationship Between Religiosity and Substance Use in African American Adolescents," *Journal of Ethnicity in Substance Abuse* 1, no. 4 (2002): 63-82.

[16]Bryon Johnson, Sung Juon Jang, David Larson and Spencer De'Li, "Does Adolescent Religious Commitment Matter? A Reexamination of the Effects of Religiosity on Delinquency," *Journal of Research in Crime and Delinquency* 38, no. 1 (2001): 22-44.

[17]Stephen Burket, "Perceived Parents' Religiosity, Friends, Drinking, and Hellfire: A Panel Study," *Review of Religious Research* 35, no. 2 (1993): 134-55.

[18]Boris Lee, Jerf Yeung and Yuk-Chung Chan, "Youth Religiosity and Substance Abuse: A Meta-Analysis from 1995-2007," *Psychological Reports* 105, no. 1 (2008): 255-66.

[19]Ian Sutherland and John Shephard, "Social Dimensions of Adolescent Substance Abuse," *Addiction* 96, no. 3 (2002): 445-58.

[20]Bettina Piko and Kevin Fitzpatrick, "Substance Use, Religiosity, and Other Protective Factors Among Hungarian Adolescents," *Addictive Behavior* 29, no. 6 (2004): 1095-1107.

[21]See Richard Munch, *Sociological Theory* (Chicago: Nelson Hall, 1994), 1:124.

[22]Andrew Cherry, *The Socializing Instincts: Individual, Family, and Social Bonds* (Westport, CT: Praeger, 1993), p. 77.

[23]Carolyn Smith, Adrienne Lozotte, Alan Thornberry and Alan Krohn, "Resilient Youth: Identifying Factors That Prevent High-Risk Youth from Engaging In Delinquency and Drug Use," *Current Perspectives on Aging and the Life Cycle* 4 (1995): 217-47.

[24]Stephen Cernkovich and Peggy Giordano, "School Bonding, Race, and Delinquency," *Criminology* 30, no. 2 (1992): 261-91.

[25]Johnson, Jang, Larson and De'Li, "Does Adolescent Religious Commitment Matter?" pp. 22-44.

[26]Hilma Granqvist, "Attachment and Religiosity in Adolescents: Cross Sectional and Longitudinal Evaluations," *Personality and Social Psychological Bulletin* 28 (2003): 260-70.

[27]Robert Corwyn and Brent Benda, "The Effect of Abuse in Childhood and in Adolescence on Violence Among Adolescents," *Youth and Society* 33, no. 3 (2002): 339-52; and Mark Regnerus and Glen Elder, "Staying on Track in School: Religious Influences in High and Low Risk Settings," *Journal for the Scientific Study of Religion* 42, no. 4 (2003): 633-49.

[28]Cydney Van Dyke and Maurice Elias, "How Forgiveness, Purpose, and Religiosity Are Related to the Mental Health and Well Being of Youth: A Review of the Literature," *Religion and Culture* 10, no. 4 (July 2007): 395-415.

[29]Ian Meltzer, Howard Dogra, Vostanis Nisha and Tamsin Ford, "Religiosity and the Mental Health of Youth in Great Britain," *Mental Health, Religion & Culture* 14, no. 7 (September 2011): 703-13.

[30]S. Huculak and J. McLennan. "The Lord Is My Shepherd: Examining Spirituality as a Protection Against Mental Health Problems in Youth Exposed to Violence in Brazil," *Mental Health, Religion, and Culture* 13, no. 5 (July 2010): 467-84

[31]The youth ministry purpose statements of the Southern Baptist Convention, Church of God, Roman Catholic, United Methodist, Episcopal, and Presbyterian Church USA denominations are described by Dean Hoge and Gregory Petrillo, "Determinants of Church Participation and Attitudes Among High School Youth," *Journal for the Scientific Study of Religion* 17, no. 4 (1978): 359-80.

[32]Lawrence Kohlberg, "Stage and Sequences of the Cognitive Development Approach to Socialization," in *Handbook of Socialization Theory and Research*, ed. David Goslin (Chicago: Rand McNally, 1969), p. 145.

[33]Kohlberg, quoted in Richard Munch, ed., *Sociological Theory* (Chicago: Nelson Hall, 1994), 3:237.

[34]Len Kageler, "A Cross National Analysis of Church Based Youth Ministries," *Journal of Youth Ministry* 8, no. 2 (2010): 49-68.

[35]Tables 6.2, 6.3 and 6.4 are from Philip Schwadel and Christian Smith, "Portraits of Protestant Teens: A Report on Teenagers in Major U.S. Denominations," Sociology Faculty Publications Paper 113 (University of Nebraska, Lincoln 2005), pp. 24, 29, 34. Used by permission. (December 10, 2012), http://digitalcommons.unl .edu/sociologyfacpub/113.

CHAPTER 7: YOUTH MINISTRY AMONG NONES AND FUNCTIONAL SYNCRETISTS

[1]See, for example, Atlantic Bridge's website at atlanticbridge.org.

[2]This may seem like youth ministry heresy, but I never give "youth talks" or "preach" at kids. It is beyond the scope of this book to unpack this further. I can only direct you to student-centered learning exemplified in Larry Richards, *Creative Bible Teaching* (Chicago: Moody Press, 1998). Likewise I religiously follow the "Seven Laws of the Teacher" found in Howard Hendricks, *Teaching to Change Lives: Seven Proven Ways to Make Your Teaching Come Alive* (Portland, OR: Multnomah Books, 2003).

[3]See, for example, Troy Beckert et al., "Single Mothers of Early Adolescents: Perceptions of Competence," *Adolescence* 43, no. 170, (2008): 275-90. In a majority of the family issues studied, the mother felt she needed a lot more help to provide an adequate home life.

[4]That can be a tall order, especially if the youth ministry budget is squeezed by churchwide revenue shortfall or other realities. In two of the three churches I served as youth pastor, that "other reality" included a no-fundraising policy applicable to all ministries of the church. (The church leadership felt that if every group in the church were raising special money for some pet project or trip, the church foyer would become akin to the temple courts from which Jesus

ejected the money changers [see Mt 21:12; Jn 2:15]. Furthermore, they did not want members of these groups raising funds in the community through door-to-door solicitations, bake sales or carwashes). Early in my ministry career I funded extra help for kids of single parents by my own tithe. In other words, I short-changed the church from time to time. Eventually, however, I obtained permission from church leadership to alter in my annual "How can I as a parent help?" survey given to parents. One item included "Give up to $75 once during the school year at the youth pastor's request to help fund a kid to do an activity or go on a retreat that their family could otherwise not afford." Thus, I had a list (usually twenty to twenty-five families) that I could go to for that one-time financial contribution.

[5]Of the many excellent resources for approaching these nones is Tim Keller, *The Reason for God: Belief in the Age of Skepticism* (New York: Dutton, 2008).

[6]Alain de Botton, *Religion for Atheists: A Non-Believer's Guide to the Uses of Religion* (New York: Pantheon, 2012).

[7]This reminds me of Paul Chamberlain's *Can We Be Good Without God?* (Downers Grove, IL: InterVarsity Press, 2001). Chamberlain answers no. A more recent work in the same vein answers yes. See Greg Epstein, *Good Without God: What a Billion Nonreligious People Do Believe* (New York: William Morrow, 2010).

[8]Christian Smith, *Souls in Transition* (New York: Oxford University Press, 2009) pp. 297-98. Smith concludes, "Religion thus makes important difference in areas of life that matter to nearly everyone and have consequences for collective well-being and social and financial costs for society as a whole. Far from having dwindled into irrelevance, religion still matters and makes a positive difference in lives of America's emerging adults" (p. 298).

[9]Which meant, "These are my boys; this is my fiefdom, my territory, and your presence is upsetting the social hierarchy here, which I won't stand for!" Undaunted, Anne continued to come and, as you can well imagine, our youth group was, well, *complicated* the remainder of that school year until our "queen" graduated from high school.

[10]We will only be discussing cognitive development as it relates to youth syncretism here. For an excellent treatment of the full range of adolescent development issues and implications, see Amy Jacober, *The Adolescent Journey* (Downers Grove, IL: InterVarsity Press, 2011).

[11]For a good and thorough review of Piaget's work see Barry Wadsworth, *Piaget's Theory of Cognitive and Affective Development*, 5th ed. (New York: Pearson, 2003).

[12]See John Medina, *Brain Rules* (Seattle: Pear Press, 2008), which discusses the prefrontal cortex. Speaking of the development of the brain the author quips, "In

short, this region [prefrontal cortex] controls many of the behaviors that separate us from other animals. And from teenagers" (ibid., p. 40).

[13]At age fourteen I entered my adolescent rebellion phase, trying to be distinct from my parents. My father was a labor leader; that is, he had a high position in a large union. By definition it meant my parents *always* voted for Democrats. We even attended a Democratic National Convention. That year, in a fit of rebellion, I took the bus downtown to the Republican headquarters and came home with a bumper sticker for the Republican Party nominee for president. I placed that sticker on my bicycle and rode around the block twice! That was my entire acting-out phase of adolescent individuation. Most would say, I think, that my parents got off pretty easy when it came to teenage rebellion.

[14]One very interesting discussion of prefrontal cortex development can be found in Po Bronson, *Nurture Shock: New Thinking About Children* (New York: Hachette, 2009). See especially chap. 9, "Plays Well with Others: Why Modern Parenting Has Failed to Produce a Generation of Angels."

[15]My answer to a young teen girl wondering about hell as the destination of her locker partner is, "We know also from the Bible that God loves every single person in the world. That's why he sent Jesus. We know also from especially the book of Acts that Christians were so loving that other people wanted to know Jesus too. Our first job is to be loving to people around us. If you'd like to talk more about this after youth group, that would be fine."

[16]See also Joseph Reimer, Diana Paolitto and Richard Hersh, *Promoting Moral Growth: From Piaget to Kohlberg* (Long Grove, IL: Waveland, 1990). A youth group may fit into their "Just-Community Approach" paradigm (ibid., p. 236).

[17]Leonard Kageler, "High School Church Youth Groups: Growth and Decline," PhD diss. (Fordham University, 2009).

[18]The figure of eighteen months as the average youth pastor tenure has always been a myth. Whenever I see the eighteen-month stat in print, I contact the author to request citation information. "I heard it somewhere" or "Everyone knows that is the number" is the normal response. The actual number is about five years, according to several studies done to high academic standards. I did a study of youth pastors who left their ministries because of being fired or due to burnout, and the average length of tenure in this group was 4.8 years. See Len Kageler, *The Youth Ministry Survival Guide* (Grand Rapids: Zondervan, 2008), p. 17.

[19]Of course I got permission from stakeholders before this. I explained and received approval from the pastoral staff, the board of elders and the parents. I clearly told parents, in the parent meeting and in written follow-up for those not at the

meeting, that if they had any discomfort with this scenario, they should not allow their child to attend Sunday school on that day. Furthermore, if their son or daughter was not able to attend the following Sunday, where we unpacked and discussed the presentation, they should not allow their child to attend the Sunday when the professor was making the presentation.

[20]If you decide to try something similar, don't skip the step of getting approval from all parties involved. This is not the kind of thing to spring on people. Another piece of advice: At first I thought it would be good to ask an atheist high school teacher to come, so I asked the students if there was one teacher at their school who stood out as not being a Christian. Confident that I had a good candidate from the number of students who identified one, I proceeded to make the phone call at the end of the school day. I was a couple of minutes into my explanation of the whole thing when he stopped me with the words "Wait, who says I'm not a Christian! You think I'm not a Christian?" Yikes, he was really upset, and it took me a long time, as you could well imagine, to extricate myself from the conversation. So, I learned it was better to call a department chair of the university, explain the nature and purpose of my call and have him or her recommend someone sure to relish the opportunity to speak to our youth. I never had a bad experience using this method of finding a speaker.

[21]Marlene Lefever, *Learning Styles* (Colorado Springs: Cook Communications, 1995).

CHAPTER 8: CHRISTIAN ENGAGEMENT WITH OTHER RELIGIONS IN YOUTH WORK

[1]The appropriateness of this point of view comes from a variety of sources. For example, Os Guinness in *In Two Minds: Christian Doubt and How to Resolve It* (Downers Grove, IL: InterVarsity Press, 1976) speaks of what he calls "Christian college doubt" (p. 79). This is doubt triggered by being sheltered from alternate points of view, which often results in a college student abandoning faith as childish. A more formal academic study on religious doubt is Keith Puffer et al., "Religious Doubt and Identity Formation: Salient Predictors of Adolescent Religious Doubt," *Journal of Psychology and Theology* 36, no. 4 (2008): 270-84. Some adolescents react negatively to constantly being told what to believe (see p. 275).

[2]Root reminds us that people are people and that God loves them all, period. We are thus doing kingdom work whenever we build a relationship with another person. See Andrew Root, *Revisiting Relational Youth Ministry* (Downers Grove, IL: InterVarsity Press, 2007), p. 15.

[3]Eboo Patel, "Living in an Age of Religious Diversity," *Neue* 10 (December–January 2012): 24.

[4]Eboo Patel, *Acts of Faith* (Boston, Beacon, 2007), p. 166. See also Eboo Patel and Patrice Brodeur, eds., *Building the Interfaith Youth Movement* (New York: Rowman & Littlefield, 2006).

[5]James Engel and Wilbert Norton, *What's Gone Wrong with the Harvest* (Grand Rapids: Zondervan, 1975), p. 53. I have adapted some of the original terminology.

[6]We even see this concept practiced by Jesus himself. For example, Mark 2:15 reports, "While Jesus was having dinner at Levi's house, many tax collectors and 'sinners' were eating with him and his disciples, for there were many who followed him." Apparently Jesus welcomed people to be with him—to belong to his community, so to speak—and eventually many of them believed in him as the Christ. It is interesting that many churches have adopted the "belong before belief" idea into their vision statements. For example, see homepage of Highland Christian Church, Asheville, https://highlandchristian.com. The concept is also discussed in Dave Browning, *Deliberate Simplicity: How the Church Does More by Doing Less,* Leadership Network Innovation Series (Grand Rapids: Zondervan, 2009), p. 74.

[7]"The Framework," Interfaith Youth Core, accessed January 17, 2013, www.ifyc.org /about.

[8]See especially chap. 1 of Patel, *Building the Interfaith Youth Movement,* p. 15. This is also the theme in his *Sacred Ground: Pluralism, Prejudice, and the Promise of America* (Boston: Beacon, 2012). Another book affirming the social benefits of interfaith relationships and activity is Robert Putnam and David Campbell, *American Grace: How Religion Divides and Unites Us* (New York: Simon & Schuster, 2012). An adult version of IFYC exists in the form of "Faith Club," founded by three women—one Jewish, one Muslim and one Christian. See Ranya Idliby, Suzanne Oliver and Priscilla Warner, *Faith Club* (New York: Free Press, 2007).

[9]See the Youth Interfaith Council website at http://youthinterfaithcouncil.org.

[10]Andrew Smith, interview by author, Birmingham, UK, February 8, 2012.

[11]"Ethical Guidelines for Christian and Muslim Witness in Britain," Christian Muslim Forum, accessed January 9, 2013, www.christianmuslimforum.org/down loads/Ethical_Guidelines_for_Witness.pdf.

[12]"After-School Programs," *Education Week,* August 3, 2004, www.edweek.org/ew /issues/after-school-programs.

[13]Heidi Rolland Unruh and Ronald J. Sider, *Saving Souls, Serving Society: Understanding the Faith Factor in Church-Based Social Ministry* (New York: Oxford University Press, 2005). Another good resource is John Perkins, *Restoring At-Risk Communities: Doing It Together and Doing It Right* (Grand Rapids: Baker, 1996).

[14]"ABC . . . 1 2 3: Starting Your Afterschool Program," Utah Department of Work-force Services, accessed January 17, 2013, www.afterschoolalliance.org/Utah 4HAfterschoolGuide.pdf.

[15]"PrimeTime," Scripture Union, accessed January 17, 2013, www.primetimeafter school.com/content/primetime%C2%AE.

[16]If a particularly heavy prayer request was voiced, I had that person kneel and we gathered around and laid hands on the person and prayed. I taught them what "laying on of hands" symbolized in the New Testament.

[17]In my interviews with Muslim youth leaders mentioned in chapter two, I often heard frustration and even despair by these youth workers over the complete disregard of young people by the mosque leadership. One Muslim youth leader in Canada exclaimed to me, "I can't stand those conservative sheikhs and imams. Don't they get it? Don't they see we are going to lose our youth?"

[18]Rick Lawrence of Group/Simply Youth Ministry expresses the same discomfort with lectures. A good summary of Rick's thinking is found at "The Problem With Youth Talks," ChurchLeaders.com, accessed January 10, 2013, www.churchleaders .com/youth/youth-leaders-how-tos/151657-the-problem-with-youth-talks.html.

[19]An excellent resource on confrontation with Satan is Chuck Davis's *Authority Encounter* (New York: Beaufort, 2013). A resource written especially for teenagers is Neil Anderson and Dave Park's *The Bondage Breaker* (Eugene, OR: Harvest House, 1993).

[20]Frank Peretti's novel *This Present Darkness* (Wheaton, IL: Crossway, 2003) helped me conceptualize the possibility of spiritual warfare.

CHAPTER 9: A MULTIFAITH PASTORAL THEOLOGY

[1]The youth rally that so concerned the letter writer went on as planned, with the unanimous support of our church elders. It was clear to those who attended that the Lord was powerfully present that night. With so much prayer from all over the country, how could it have been otherwise? Interestingly, though there was no invitation to receive Christ given that night, two students made known to us that they crossed the line into faith that night.

[2]Richard Dunn and Mark Senter III, *Reaching a Generation for Christ* (Chicago: Moody Press, 1997), p. 51.

[3]Ibid., p. 65.

[4]Kenda Dean, Chap Clark and David Rahn, eds., *Starting Right: Thinking Theologically About Youth Ministry* (Grand Rapids: Zondervan, 2001).

[5]Andrew Root and Kenda Creasy Dean, *The Theological Turn in Youth Ministry*

(Downers Grove, IL: InterVarsity Press, 2011). They first lay a theological foundation, unpacking their belief that all youth ministry is ultimately theological in nature. I especially love Kenda's chapter "Ascension Deficit Disorder: Youth Ministry as a Laboratory for Hope."

[6]Mike King, *Presence-Centered Youth Ministry* (Downers Grove, IL: InterVarsity Press, 2006). In this same stream is the work by Kenda Creasy Dean and Ron Foster, *The Godbearing Life: The Art of Soul Tending in Youth Ministry* (Nashville: Upper Room, 2005).

[7]Mark Yaconelli, *Contemplative Youth Ministry* (Grand Rapids: Zondervan, 2006).

[8]Rick Lawrence, *Jesus-Centered Youth Ministry* (Loveland, CO: Group, 2007). Rick additionally cites the *Study of Exemplary Congregations in Youth Ministry*, finding the commonality of "Jesus first" in these ministries. See www.exemplarym.com.

[9]The ancient and medieval Christian creeds tried to find appropriate language for Christ's divine and human natures. "Very God and very man" comes from the Westminster Confession of Faith, published in 1646, which includes several paragraphs about the person and work of Christ. In the third paragraph we find "So that two whole, perfect, and distinct natures, the Godhead and the manhood, were inseparably joined together in one person, without conversion, composition or confusion. Which person is *very God and very man*, yet one Christ, the only Mediator between God and man."

[10]The phrase "in and out" was familiar to Jesus' hearers. It was metaphor for peaceful and safe passage in life. The scaffolding erected by the religious leaders of the day was intended to assure that following them was the only way people could earn access to God or find favor with God. For example, in John 9:13-34 we see the Pharisees investigating a healing that was getting very good press. Jesus' rising popularity was a threat to their place as gatekeepers. In John 9:22 the parents of the healed son are clearly intimidated as they mince their words during the investigation. Additionally, C. Barclay suggests that Jesus may have had in mind also those who considered themselves leaders, the Zealots. The Zealot answer for how to have a good life and ensure secure "in and out" was to participate in armed insurrection against the Romans. See Charles Barclay, *The Gospel According to John*, vol. 2 (Philadelphia: Westminister, 1955) p. 68.

[11]There is robust scholarly interest in altruism and happiness, especially altruism that is motivated by religious faith. For example, see Anne Pressi, "Religiosity and Altruism: Exploring the Link and Its Relation to Happiness," *Journal of Contemporary Religion* 26, no. 1 (2011): 1-18. A more popular treatment of the personal happiness is Gretchen Rubin, *The Happiness Project* (New York: Harper, 2011).

Rubin's book has spent its first two years since publication on the *New York Times* bestseller list.

[12]I love how Andrew Root expresses this concept: "Reality is constituted by social relationships because person-to-person encounter is the pattern of Jesus' ministry, for he is ontologically *pro*-me. The place of Jesus' concrete presence calls persons to encounter persons in actions of vicarious love, and in so doing partake in the eschatological mission of God, which is to return humanity to humanity in the new humanity of Jesus Christ. Therefore, to be in the new humanity is to join in bonds of relationship (constituted solely by the person of Christ) which meet the other (my neighbor) as a transcendent mystery" (Andrew Root, *Revisiting Relational Youth Ministry* [Downers Grove, IL: InterVarsity Press, 2007], p. 173).

[13]Watchman Nee, *The Normal Christian Life* (Wheaton, IL: Tyndale House, 1957), p. 164.

[14]John Acuff, speech at the Simply Youth Ministry Conference, Indianapolis, March 2, 2013.

[15]Two books that try to convey who we are in Christ in a very youth-friendly format are both by Neil T. Anderson and David Park: *The Bondage Breaker: Youth Edition* (Eugene, OR: Harvest House, 2006), and *Stomping Out the Darkness* (Los Angeles: Regal, 2008).

[16]A good example is found in Brian Belton and Sadek Hamid, eds., *Youth Work and Islam* (Rotterdam: Sense Publishers, 2012), p. 102.

[17]See Richard Kammerer, "Suffering: The Missing Element in Contemporary Christology," *Youth Worker*, September 1, 2006, www.youthworker.com/youth-ministry-resources-ideas/youth-ministry/11552633.

[18]Rodney Stark, *The Rise of Christianity* (Princeton, NJ: Princeton University Press, 1996), p. 163. Stark posits Christian reaction to persecution as one of the three main reasons Christianity grew in the first three hundred years of the church. The other two main reasons are that Christians did not practice abortion and they helped people in plague time.

[19]Keith Miller, *The Taste of New Wine* (Waco, TX: 1965), p. 94.

[20]C. S. Lewis, *The Problem of Pain* (San Francisco: Harper, 2001), p. 3. Rick Lawrence makes a similar point: "Name something that captures your heart that was not formed by pain" (Rick Lawrence, *Sifted* [Colorado Springs: David C. Cook, 2011], p. 30).

IVP PRAXIS

EQUIPPING LEADERS FOR MINISTRY

"...TO EQUIP HIS PEOPLE FOR WORKS OF SERVICE,

SO THAT THE BODY OF CHRIST MAY BE BUILT UP."

EPHESIANS 4:12

God has called us to ministry. But it's not enough to have a vision for ministry if you don't have the practical skills for it. Nor is it enough to do the work of ministry if what you do is headed in the wrong direction. We need both vision *and* expertise for effective ministry. We need *praxis*.

Praxis puts theory into practice. It brings cutting-edge ministry expertise from visionary practitioners. You'll find sound biblical and theological foundations for ministry in the real world, with concrete examples for effective action and pastoral ministry. Praxis books are more than the "how to" – they're also the "why to." And because *being* is every bit as important as *doing*, Praxis attends to the inner life of the leader as well as the outer work of ministry. Feed your soul, and feed your ministry.

If you are called to ministry, you know you can't do it on your own. Let Praxis provide the companions you need to equip God's people for life in the kingdom.

www.ivpress.com/praxis